JACKASSERY

Learn How To Achieve Success By Vaccinating Yourself Against This Wealth-Destroying Disease

D1600592

BY CLAY CLARK

Jackassery: Learn How to Achieve Success by Vaccinating Yourself
Against This Wealth-Destroying Disease
ISBN 978-0-9984435-0-8
Copyright © 2016 by Clay Clark

Thrive Publishing

Published by Thrive Publishing
1100 Suite #100 Riverwalk Terrace
Jenks, OK 74037

TABLE OF CONTENTS

Statue of limitations vs. Statute of limitations

Early on in my business career, I specifically remember asking an attorney if I could still prosecute someone or if we had reached the "statue of limitations." Unfortunately, I did not yet understand that a "statue" is a carved or cast figure, while a "statute" is a written law passed by a legislative body. Now that I understand that subtle difference, I try aggressively to avoid referencing the sculpture of limitations.

INTRODUCTION

"We are all born ignorant, but one must work hard to remain stupid."

~ Benjamin Franklin ~
One of the Founding Fathers of the United States of America;
successful author, printer, politician, postmaster, diplomat; renowned
inventor of bifocals, the lighting rod and the Franklin stove, and kind
of a big deal.

AMPLE EXAMPLES OF JACKASSERY ALL AROUND US

"75% of employees steal from the workplace and...most do so repeatedly."

Rich Russakoff and Mary Goodman, "Employee Theft: Are You Blind to It?" CBS News Moneywatch, July 14, 2011, http://www.cbsnews. com/news/employee-theft-are-you-blind-to-it/.

"15 to 20% of the U.S. population is 'consistently late,' especially when it comes to work."

ABC News. "Running Late and Wasting Billions," March 3, 2007, http:// abcnews.go.com/GMA/story?id=2920989.

"The average American watches more than five hours of live television every day."

David Hinckley, "Average American watches 5 hours of TV per day, report shows," New York Daily News, March 5, 2014, http://www. nydailynews.com/life-style/average-american-watches-5-hours-tv- day-article-1.1711954.

"Gallup's data shows 30% of employees Engaged, 52% Disengaged, 18% Actively Disengaged. These latest findings indicate that 70% of American workers are "not engaged" or "actively disengaged" and are emotionally disconnected from their workplaces and less likely to be productive.'"

Victor Lipman, "Surprising, Disturbing Facts From The Mother Of All Employee Engagement Surveys," Forbes, September 23, 2013, http:// www.forbes.com/sites/victorlipman/2013/09/23/surprising-disturbing- facts-from-the-mother-of-all-employee-engagement-surveys/.

"88% of wealthy read 30 minutes or more each day for education or career reasons vs. 2% of poor."

"20 Things the Rich Do Every Day," list compiled by Dave Ramsey from information found in Rich Habits – Daily Success Habits of Wealthy Individuals by Thomas C. Corley (Minneapolis, MN: Langdon Street Press, 2010). http://www.daveramsey.com/blog/20-things-the-rich- do-every-day.

"Children in father-absent homes are almost four times more likely to be poor. In 2011, 12 percent of children in married-couple families were living in poverty, compared to 44 percent of children in mother-only families."

U.S. Census Bureau, "Children's Living Arrangements and Characteristics," March 2011, Table C8. Washington, D.C.

"One out of every three (children in America), live in biological father-absent homes. Nine in ten American parents agree this is a 'crisis'."

National Father Initiative, "There is a 'Father Factor' in Our Nation's Worst Social Problems," Fatherhood.org, http://www.fatherhood.org/father-absence-statistics.

My friend, according to research conducted by Thomas C. Corley, CPA, certified financial planner and bestselling author of the book Rich Habits: The Daily Success Habits of Wealthy Individuals and published on DaveRamsey.com, "88% of wealthy (people) read 30 minutes or more each day for education or career reasons versus 2% of the poor." Corley's research also reveals that 86% of the wealthy believe in lifelong educational self-improvement versus 5% of the poor (http://www.daveramsey.com/blog/20-things-the-rich-do-every-day).

When I first read this information, it made my brain almost explode. As a former advocate for the idiocracy form of government and former practitioner of the dark art of jackassery, these stats now seem obvious. But back in the day when I was still focused on installing subwoofers into my Mazda MPV minivan and seeing how many soft, salted buttery pretzels I could eat during my shifts working at Target, I had no idea how much of a jackass I was. I was dumb, but I too busy trying to keep up with the storyline of Survivor and the East Coast / West Coast rap feud to recognize that I was quickly going nowhere.

Fast forward to today...

Now, as a former U.S. Small Business Administration Entrepreneur of the Year, father of five kids, consultant to some of America's top companies, speaker, author, owner of multiple businesses and founder of Thrive15.com, people often ask me:

- How can I go from financially just surviving to thriving?
- How do I start a business?
- How can I grow my business?
- How can I advance in my career?
- What do I need to do to raise capital?
- How do I write a business plan?
- How do I improve my company's sales?
- How can I get featured in the media?
- How do I learn to manage my time better?

- How can I learn to better manage my people?
- How do I optimize my website?
- What are your keys to success?
- When do you find time to sleep?
- How many hours per day do you sleep?
- Why are you so pale?
- Are you aware of what causes pregnancy?

As I begin to answer their questions, I find myself wishing it was actually possible to hop into a time machine so I could go back in time and rescue myself from the world of jackassery I lived in for so long. If I could only go back and coach my younger self on how not to be a jackass, on how to just say no to the five hours of TV per day that the average American watches and that I once enjoyed, my world would have been different. I find myself wishing that Doc Brown's time-traveling DeLorean from Back to the Future was real so that I could go back and force myself to read 30 minutes per day like 88% of millionaires do. If I could just do that, I know my life would have become much better, much faster. But unfortunately, this is not possible and, according to Doc Brown, probably not advisable anyway:

"I foresee two possibilities. One, seeing herself thirty years in the future would put Jennifer into shock and she'd simply pass out. Or two, the encounter could create a time paradox. The results of which could cause a chain reaction that would unravel the very fabric of the space-time continuum and destroy the entire universe!...Granted, that's the worst-case scenario."

However, all things considered, if I could go back in time and save myself from jackassery, I would risk everything to do it because frankly, success is not very hard to achieve if you know what you are doing and if you aren't setting yourself on fire by practicing the dark art known as jackassery.

"Ample examples of Jackassery are all around us if we will just look within our deeper selves." - Clay Clark (Recovering avid practitioner of Jackassery)

A Clarification for Those Who Have Never Personally Practiced Jackassery...

If you have never practiced jackassery, you may be asking yourself, "What is jackassery?"

Well, my friend, the word "jackassery" comes from the root word "jackass." The good folks at Merriam-Webster define a "jackass" as:

1. A person who lacks good sense or judgment.

2. A stupid person.

3. A sturdy and patient domestic mammal that is used especially to carry things.

At one point in time, I think I would have said definition #3 applied to me. However, as one of the leading experts and authorities on the subject of jackassery (having once been a practitioner of the dark art), I define "jackassery" as the type of activity that a highly-motivated, sincere and oblivious idiot often engages in. Perhaps an example will help you get the picture. Once upon a time in 1999, I was completely controlled by the habit force of jackassery to the point that I had almost become a mindless drone, unable to engage in rational thought for more than thirty seconds. I dressed like Eminem (the super-skilled Caucasian rapper), wore Wu-Tang Clan (the rap group) T-shirts, sported large double hoop earrings and I always suggested my potential wedding entertainment clients meet me at McDonald's for a face-to-face sales presentation. For some reason I thought I would have success convincing a bride-to-be and her mother to pay me 600 to 1,000 of their hard-earned dollars to be their wedding entertainment of choice, when everything about me suggested that I would be participating in a convenience store robbery immediately following our meeting at McDonald's. The power of jackassery had such a strong hold on my life that it never occurred to me that the bride-to-be was planning to spend $25,000 to turn her wedding dreams into reality at an event that was going to be attended by her closest family and friends and perhaps, she might be looking for an entertainer who exuded fewer tendencies of jackassery.

Jackassery has a different effect on everyone, but for me, it gave me super physical flexibility and extremely limited mental dexterity. My spine was able to bend in such a way that at times, I was actually able to place my head so deep inside my own rectal cavity that I became completely unaware of my surroundings. As a coping mechanism, I've learned to block out those memories. However, people tell me that I actually conducted every sales meeting - for over one year, mind you - at McDonald's without the benefit of having any marketing materials, brochures, print pieces or contracts. Apparently, I also shunned the use of a briefcase, preferring to just store my paperwork in my backpack.

As I reminisce on this dark period in my life, I can clearly remember my mantra at the time: "Only God can judge me." This mentality was perfect because it combined references to my Judeo-Christian upbringing and to the new American religion of not judging others. It also allowed me to pass blame when I failed to close the sale as brides, mothers of brides, event planners and anyone with a functional mind consistently refused to book me. My "only God can judge me" mantra was one of my justifications for struggling. I blamed the economy, I blamed the closed-

This photo features me (left) at a Casino with my best friend Mark (right) celebrating my complete devotion to jackassery.

minded culture and I blamed the judgmental potential customers. This mentality was my way of clinging to one of the foundational tenets of jackassery: "Thou shalt not 'sell out,' even if it means never selling one's products or services and a near certain guarantee of a lifetime of poverty."

My friends, I was so actively engaged in jackassery that such behavior became my normal. I had been mentored by some of the world's elite jackasses and I just knew that jackassery was the path for me.

Had the pursuit of millions not driven me to millionaire mentors who changed my mindset, I would still be a jackass today. Looking back, it's amazing how similar nearly every millionaire mentor I've ever had truly is, regardless of their age, race or gender.

- They nearly all carry a to-do list either on paper or in digital form.
- They are all relentless learners.
- They all block off nearly one hour per day to be alone to plan and engage in strategic thinking.
- They all have a day-planner.
- They all believe that they can create their own luck.
- They are all intentional about surrounding themselves with successful people.
- They all have intense work ethics and laugh at the notion that one can achieve success by adhering to President Roosevelt's Fair Labor Standards Act of 1938, which limited the standard workweek to 44 hours. I remember the look on one mentor's exasperated face when she said to me, "You mean that it took God six days to create the earth, but you believe you can create your millions working 9 to 5? Look honey, if you want to be a successful entrepreneur, you can work whatever 80 hours per week you choose."
- They are very intentional about what thoughts they allow into their minds. Therefore, they don't watch copious amounts of mindless television or listen to hours upon hours of hip-hop musicians rapping about sex and drugs.

The Evolution of a Recovering Jackass

"After you become a millionaire, you can give all of your money away because what's important is not the million dollars; what's important is the person you have become in the process of becoming a millionaire."

~ Jim Rohn (Bestselling author, speaker and one of the founders of the modern self-help movement) ~

Thinking back on my days of jackassery, I realize I was intentionally doing all the things that they were intentionally NOT doing.

- I wrote everything down on post-it notes, yellow legal pads, wadded up pieces of paper, the backs of receipts and anything else I was guaranteed to lose.

- I was 100% committed to not learning, because I already knew it all. Life was just a matter of "common sense."

- I could not handle spending any time alone. I made sure that I was always surrounded by people and their mindless chatter.

- I had no idea where I was supposed to be or when I was supposed to be there.

- I believed that "it takes money to make money" and that "the rich get richer."

- I was intentional about surrounding myself with as many aspiring rappers as possible.

- I thought that anyone who worked more than 40 hours per week was a "workaholic." I believed that I needed at least one unscheduled day off per three weeks to "make sure that I don't get burned out."

- I usually turned on the television and watched whatever was on. Whenever I hopped into my sub-woofer enhanced Mazda MPV, I listened to the Chronic 2001 album by Dr. Dre or Eminem's The Real Slim Shady, because I wanted to make sure I was filling my mind with music about sex, drugs, dysfunctional relationships, and violence.

Thankfully, today I have been cured of those terrible wealth-repelling habits. Although, like a mosquito is attracted to a bug zapper, I find myself tempted to return to a few of those habits from time to time. At times like that, I give thanks that my wife is smarter than I am and that I am now influenced by people who are far more successful than me.

As I have relentlessly pursued the coaching, teaching and mentorship of some of the world's most successful people including David Robinson, Lee Cockerell, Michael Levine, Clifton Taulbert, Doctor Robert Zoellner and countless others with everyday entrepreneurial success stories, my normal has been redefined. I now have a burning passion to save the world from this wealth-destroying-drifting-through-life-in-a-near-comatose-I-hope-to-win-the-lottery-showing-up-for-work-late-only-saving-money-when-i-need-a-new-tattoo-dream-reducing-addictive-habit-force I have officially named "jackassery."

It blows my mind that this former avid practitioner of the wealth-repelling habits listed above now spends his weeks traveling around the world recording practical business skill and mindset training with the world's most successful people. Simply changing my mindset and my habits changed everything for me. I am now so blessed to interview gurus and millionaire mentors like...

- David Robinson (NBA Hall of Fame basketball player turned entrepreneur and founder of the Carver Academy charter school and the $300 million dollar Admiral Capital Group).

- Lee Cockerell (Former Executive Vice President of Operations for Walt Disney World Resort, who once managed over 40,000 employees / cast members).

- Michael Levine (Bestselling author and the public relations consultant of choice for Nike, Pizza Hut, Michael Jackson, 58 Academy Award

Winners, 34 Grammy Award Winners and 42 New York Times Best Sellers).

- Clifton Taulbert (Bestselling author of Once Upon a Time When We Were Colored, which was turned into a major motion picture of the same name that Siskel and Ebert rated "two thumbs up").

- Doctor Robert Zoellner (Successful optometrist turned entrepreneur and the founder / partner of Z66 Auto Auction, Rockin' Z' Ranch, Dr ZZZs Sleep Center, Robert H. Zoellner and Associates and Thrive15. com).

My friends, whether you choose to believe in the destructive powers of this supernatural success repulsion system or not, the power of jackassery is all around you. Jackassery is what gives a poverty mindset its power. *"It's an energy field created by all living things. It surrounds us. It penetrates us. It binds the galaxy together."* – Ben Obi Wan-Kenobi

As a testament to how small my mind is, I often chose to take photos with the worst possible camera, as evidenced by the photo above. Despite my inadequacies, I have emerged from the habit force of jackassery. This picture features from left to right, Thrive15.com CEO Robert Zoellner, Regent Bank Owner and CEO Sean Kouplen, NBA Hall of Famer turned entrepreneurial success story David Robinson, me, and the web-designer of choice for Garth Brooks and countless other big-time project managers Jason Stewart.

Jackassery Is Happening in Your City Right Now

In an article written by Tami Luhby for CNNMoney titled, "The American Dream is out of reach" (http://money.cnn.com/2014/06/04/news/economy/american-dream/), it is reported that 59% of the Americans surveyed said that the American Dream (however they define it) is out of reach. As a recovering practitioner of jackassery, I find this hard to believe. I think far more Americans believe that their dream life is out of reach.

I vividly remember a time in my life when I sincerely believed that success was just a matter of luck. I remember when I had zero time in my schedule to study how to build a website or how to grow a business, because I was way too busy trying to decipher all of the coded messages hidden within the lyrical miracles of famous rappers. I used to believe that Christopher Wallace (a.k.a. Notorious B.I.G., a.k.a. Biggie Smalls) and 2Pac (a.k.a. Tupac Shakur) were modern day prophets and martyrs for positive social change. These men cleverly wove the most complicated and important messages into their songs (or so I thought) and I just had to know what their lyrics really meant. Their lyrics were the Jackass Magna Carta. They spoke to me and as I listened, I actually took notes. As I recall this dark time in my life, I'm literally laughing out loud at my past behavior to avoid crying over so much wasted opportunity.

You see, fully understanding rap lyrics takes time, like aging a fine wine. It takes time to find the kernels of universal truth in those masterpieces, kind of like the time it takes to pick kernels of corn out of dog excrement. I simply had no time to study how to communicate and maximize my time, because I was busy decoding lyrics. I did not have time to learn how to raise capital because I was literally writing my senior paper on such deep subjects as the life and times of the late Tupac Shakur. This is my true history and I must face it.

It Takes Commitment and Hours of Time to Really Understand Rap Lyrics

If you have never tried to memorize and decipher rap lyrics so that you can be 2% cooler when you go out dancing with your friends, you just can't possibly understand the level of commitment to the dark art of jackassery it takes. To really memorize, unpack and understand an audio treasure like Notorious B.I.G.'s Top 40 hit "Juicy," it takes at least 20 hours of focused time and I'm not the kind of person who wants to do anything halfway.

My unwavering commitment to decoding rap lyrics left me with no time available to achieve the American dream and for a moment, it actually began to change my very definition of the American Dream. My friend, it takes time to learn another version of the English language, such as is used to comprise these rap masterpieces. It truly takes focus if you are to become accustomed to the overall lack of punctuation and tact and abject disregard for all rules of grammar and spelling. You can't just adjust your mental temperature quickly. It requires hours upon hours of listening for you to allow this language filled with grammatical sabbaticals, hate, sex, violence, sex and more sex to become your new normal.

YOUNG DJ CLAYVIS...
1999, AGE 18

The college I attended and was subsequently kicked out of, Oral Roberts University, could require me to wear a tie, but they couldn't require me to not be dumb.

Analyze this photo and notice the large wad of cash I have in my hands, the prison shirt I am wearing, the baggy pants I have on and the cigar in my mouth. I'm sure this did not cause any members of the law enforcement community to judge me in any way.

It Takes an Investment of Time to Change Your Definition of Normal

When you've been constantly told by the leaders of the free world that you should concern yourself with proper spelling and grammar while refraining from massive quantities of cursing, elicit sex and completely uninhibited drug use, at first rap lyrics can be shocking and even off-putting. I've heard people express that they felt "dirty" and needed to take a shower after first encountering the lyrics to their favorite Top 40 rap song. But if you will just take to heart the Emperor's advice from Star Wars, "Use your aggressive feelings, boy. Let the hate flow through you," what you hear in rap lyrics will quickly become your new normal.

Allow Me to Break Down a Lyrical Miracle into Its Most Simplistic Form

My friend, let me now demonstrate the extent of my once complete mastery of the dark art of jackassery. I shall now decipher for you what one of the verses of Notorious B.I.G.'s smash hit rap song "Juicy," means in great clarity. Before you begin reading, prepare yourself for a life-changing experience. I want to caution you, however. Understanding these lyrics will decrease your overall intelligence quotient by 2%.

Because Biggie Smalls (a.k.a. Christopher Wallace, a.k.a. Notorious B.I.G.) and Puff Daddy (a.k.a. P. Diddy, a.k.a. Puff, a.k.a. Diddy, a.k.a. Sean Combs) did not play instruments, they both put their focus on the writing of mind-blowing lyrics that they hoped would have the power to advance culture in the way that the writings of Plato and Socrates have. However, what they actually created were lyrics that devolved culture by 4% and made being dumb cool again. In the world of jackassery, these men are revered as philosophers, prophets and leaders of the idiocracy movement that encourages fathers to abandon their families, drug dealers to justify their business models and the average person to be just a little less intelligent than they've ever been. Let the games begin!

Juicy

Performed by Biggie Smalls (a.k.a. Christopher Wallace, a.k.a. Notorious B.I.G.) and Puff Daddy (a.k.a. P. Diddy, a.k.a. Puff, a.k.a. Diddy, a.k.a. Sean Combs).

I made the change from a common thief

To up close and personal with Rob Leach

Translation: Christopher is explaining to us that he once was a common thief, but now he has become friends with the host of the popular show, Lifestyles of the Rich and Famous.

And I'm far from cheap, I smoke skunk with my peeps all day

Spread love, it's the Brooklyn way

Translation: When Christopher was poor he had to live very cheaply; now he has moved far away from that practice. Because of his deep religious commitment to the dark art of jackassery, he now buys expensive material things ensuring that he will remain poor, despite his massive increase in income. But he wants to let you know that the acquisition of wealth has not caused him to stop smoking marijuana. In fact, he is now smoking the really cheap marijuana that is commonly referred to as "skunk" because it literally smells like a skunk when you smoke it. He concludes this couplet by saying hello to his friends and family members who live in Brooklyn.

The Moet and Alize keep me pissy, girls used to diss me

Now they write letters 'cause they miss me

Translation: Christopher is explaining to us that he has to urinate a lot because he is drinking so much alcohol. In fact some of his favorite alcoholic beverages include Moet and Alize, which are known in the projects as "girly" drinks. He lets us all know that females used to disrespect him due to his massive physical size and the fact that he was a high school dropout who was engaged in the buying, selling and using of drugs. At one point, Christopher had to spend some time in jail in Brooklyn, New York, for weapons charges. While serving his time in jail, he claims that females used to write him encouraging letters.

I never thought it could happen, this rappin' stuff

I was too used to packin' gats and stuff

Translation: Christopher never thought that he would become a successful rap star because the life of drug peddling he was used to necessitated the carrying of handguns ("gats" – a reference to the Gatling guns which were famously used by gangsters during the time of Al Capone). However, when he was released from jail in 1992, an editor at The Source magazine heard a demo that featured Christopher. The editor was so impressed by Christopher's lyrical delivery style that he featured him in the "Unsigned Hype" column of the magazine. Soon, word of mouth spread around New York City and the young producer Puff Daddy became aware of Christopher's talents. Soon thereafter, Puff Daddy signed Christopher Wallace to Bad Boy records.

The Average American Watches Five Hours of TV Per Day

In a super-motivational article by David Hinckley that appeared in the New York Daily News titled, "The Average American watches 5 hours of TV per day," it is revealed that research conducted by Nielsen shows that the average American does in fact watch five hours of TV per day. I find this hard to believe. In my mind, the average should be way higher than five hours.

Nugget of Knowledge:
When you find yourself in a hole, it's best to stop digging.

As a former jackass who used "I didn't have time" as my prime excuse for why I wasn't able to get things done, I know that at one point, I watched way more than five hours of TV per day, especially when you count my non-stop playing of video games. When you add the number of hours I spent playing video games and watching TV to the massive amount of time I spent memorizing rap lyrics and deciphering their hidden meanings, the total is astronomical. I can't believe I ever had time to sleep. But then again, I was serious about my craft and dedicated to going nowhere as quickly as possible.

Traveling Back in Time Is Out of the Question, So I'll Just Write Myself a Few Letters

Out of respect for you and the rest of humanity, I don't want to risk creating what Doc Brown described as a "time paradox - the results of which could cause a chain reaction that would unravel the very fabric of the space-time continuum and destroy the entire universe," so I've decided to just simply write brutally honest and encouraging letters to my former self. I'm hoping that the publication of these letters might help someone out there, even as it proves to be somewhat humiliating to me.

Let's begin the beatings until morale improves...

Nugget of Knowledge: "Where there is a whip, there is a way." - Pre-politically correct livestock owners and ranchers everywhere.

THE AMERICAN DREAM IS POSSIBLE IF YOU AREN'T WATCHING TV FIVE HOURS PER DAY

At 9:09 AM, a tattooed and shirtless Ed leaves for his 9:00 AM job interview. His concerned roommate shares his #1 concern is that his gas cap is open.

Dear 14-Year-Old Clay,

I'm excited about your success. I'm glad to hear that your t-shirt business is going well and that you are starting to make a few hundred dollars per week. I'm also excited that Principal Johnson graciously decided not to expel you from the Dassel-Cokato Middle School dance - at which you were hired to perform - for inciting the literal riot that ensued. However, we need to talk.

Recently, you've decided to start dressing like Eminem and you've been investing copious amounts of time into the memorization and deciphering of rap lyrics. Although this may be a good idea if you are going to pursue a rap career, we both know that's not where you're headed. Vast accumulations of hip hop knowledge will not help you achieve the success you seek. Furthermore, your Timberland boots, super baggy jeans, double hoop earrings and massive investment in silver jewelry are beginning to repel real opportunities and women of virtue.

I realize that you love to say, "Only God can judge me," however, that is simply not true. People are currently judging you based on what you look like, what skills you have, whom you associate with, how you talk and the overall image you choose to project. Currently, you look like a hooligan or the friendliest member of a gang. You are not working to meet the right people; rather you choose to hang out with idiots who sell marijuana and who are plotting ways to have sex with the head football coach's daughter. You have minimal skills, you talk like you are working as a full-time English-to-hip-hop interpreter, and you scare old people with that facial expression you carry during 90% of your waking hours that screams, "Don't step on my shoes or I will punch you in the face!"

I know that you do not currently make a practice of reading anything other than rap lyrics, The Source magazine and SLAM magazine, but please invest the five minutes it takes to read the statistics below and see if you can draw any conclusions about what these numbers mean. An author from the future named Tom Corley has compiled these statistics. You'll be able to find these numbers about ten years from now on RichHabitsInstitute.com. Calm down. In the future, the speed of your Internet connection will be 1,000 times faster.

- 88% of wealthy read 30 minutes or more each day for education or career reasons vs. 2% of poor (The three hours per day you currently spend deciphering and memorizing rap lyrics does not count as reading for education or career reasons. And no, the senior paper that you are writing about the life and times of Tupac does not count, either.)

- 6% of wealthy say what's on their mind vs. 69% of poor (Talking trash to gang members at the gas station in Minneapolis was not a good idea and could have resulted in your death. Although you might have seen the humor in cursing out the Littlefield Dragons' mascot during your basketball game the other night, no one else did.)

- 86% of wealthy believe in lifelong educational self-improvement vs. 5% of poor (I realize that, because of your maniacal obsession with watching TV, playing video games and decoding rap lyrics, you think you are too busy to read about successful people and to study their wealth creating habits so that you can apply their principles in your own life. It's OK, my friend. You are just suffering from a mental disorder called "jackassery.")

- 63% of wealthy listen to audio books during their commute to work vs. 5% of poor people (Although both the Notorious B.I.G. and Tupac have been quoted in The Source magazine as saying that they just want to tell the truth and the stories of their lives through the rap lyrics they write, rap music cannot actually be classified as audio books.)

- 84% of wealthy believe good habits create opportunity luck vs. 4% of poor (I realize that you currently see no relationship between the way you dress and the way people treat and perceive you. I realize that in your mind, it's completely rational to sleep in every Saturday until noon. However, these habits are keeping you from the achievement of your goals and pulling you deeper into the practice of jackassery, where every committed member of the club makes at least 50% less than non-practicioners.)

- 67% of wealthy watch one hour or less of TV every day vs. 23% of poor (I realize that you have not been instructed in the Law of Cause and Effect. I understand that because of your teacher's insistence on teaching you about chlorophyll, papyrus, the Mesopotamian River

Valley and other subjects that you feel are a complete waste of time, you now associate learning with wasting time and turn to MTV as a refuge after a long day spent memorizing stuff that doesn't matter. However, you need to turn off the TV - if that is even physically possible after you just consumed six Mountain Dews at one sitting.)

- 81% of wealthy maintain a to-do list vs. 19% of poor (I know that time management and organization skills are not taught by your teachers at all, but listen to me, man. In the future, your ability to actually get things done and to keep your life organized using this thing called a "to-do list" are the only things that matter in the workplace.)

- 67% of wealthy write down their goals vs. 17% of poor (I think it may be a little scary to actually see on paper your current life goals, due to the fact that rap music is probably your only inspiration at this time. However, in the future you will become friends with millionaires as part of your job as the Chief Operating Officer at www.Thrive15.com and guess what...every millionaire you will meet maintains a "to-do" list, while the rest of the population does not. Do you see any patterns forming here? Those folks have real goals for self-development to help them advance.)

- 79% of wealthy network five hours or more each month vs. 16% of poor (Ok, I can't write this next part to you unless you 100% believe that I am, in fact, your future self and I'm just trying to help you. Look, your favorite baseball player's middle name is Nuschler. It's William Nuschler Clark. Who else would know that? Now, if you believe me, listen up. Who you know and people's impression of you will determine how much money you make. I repeat, WHO YOU KNOW AND PEOPLE'S IMPRESSION OF YOU WILL DETERMINE HOW MUCH MONEY YOU MAKE. You currently dress like a jackass and only know jackasses. Change this immediately and your life will begin improving dramatically.)

- 76% of wealthy believe bad habits create detrimental luck vs. 9% of poor (Ok, let me ask you this question and be honest with your answer: If you took the time to study successful people and began to do what they do on a daily basis, would you become more successful or less successful? I'm just asking.)

Clay, hang in there. Life is tough, challenging and dramatic when you dress like an idiot, listen to music written by idiots, hang around idiots and don't invest the 30 minutes needed every day to study how to improve your skills. However, I have some good news for you. In the future, this will all change almost overnight once you begin dressing for success and the way you want to be addressed, listening to inspiring music instead of hate-filled lyrics, hanging around quality people and investing the time needed to study success.

Sincerely, You in 15 Years,

Clay Clark

P.S. According to a Nielsen TV study, the average American of the future is currently watching nearly five hours of TV per day, so don't beat yourself up too much. You aren't the only human practicing the dark art of jackassery.

P.S. (again) - Your wife of the future is attractive and your five kids are incredible little humans.

THE PRESIDENTIAL PHOTOGRAPHY GUESSING GAME.

Instructions: Circle the picture of the person you think is the President of the Future.

CHAPTER 2

DON'T LET FORMAL EDUCATION GET IN THE WAY OF ACTUAL LEARNING

"Don't let schooling interfere with your education."

~ Mark Twain ~

Dear Clay,

I'm glad to see that you survived high school and have successfully made it into college at Oral Roberts University. I know you currently disagree with the theology being taught at this charismatic Christian university, but I think we can all agree that your actually making it into college is, in itself, a miracle of Biblical proportions. The fact that you escaped arrest and conviction for throwing eggs at police cars as they drove by while you were perched on top of the local community bank is truly miraculous, right up there with walking on water and the parting of the Red Sea, in the opinion of my 2015 mind. My friend and younger self, there had to be some divine intervention at work when those gang members you taunted in that St. Cloud, Minnesota, gas station decided not to kill you. Truly, the fact that you are alive and not in jail is miraculous and all the proof I need to believe in the presence of a higher power. Likewise, it's a modern miracle that, although you took Algebra three times and required CPR courses numerous times without ever actually passing, you still graduated from Dassel-Cokato High School in Minnesota. My friend, we also have to give thanks to the Almighty that on your third attempt, you were finally able to earn a score on your ACT high enough to get you into college.

However, Clay, the dark forces of jackassery are now beginning to take root in your life. I know that you are starting to hate learning as a result of the great four-year memorization party game called college. I know that the apathetic professors who take attendance in your social science or humanities classes filled with 300 students are making you believe that you actually dislike learning. I know that these proud syllabus-toting professors want to convince you that they can determine your potential based solely on your ability to read large portions of text and memorize meaningless facts in a way that allows you to regurgitate (vomit) the words onto a piece of paper called a test. You are beginning to feel as though learning is a waste of time. However, nothing could be further from the truth.

Jackassery in action. Armed with a semi-strong throwing arm and massive amounts of directionless ambition, a young Clay Clark attempts to hit police cars with eggs from his snow-covered perch atop the local community bank.

Your ability to learn practical business skills is going to ultimately determine your ability to earn. Listen to what a couple of history's great minds have to say about education.

- Albert Einstein, one of the planet's most famous inventors and scientists, once said, "It's a miracle that curiosity survives formal education."

- Peter Thiel, the man who will eventually start a wildly successful company of the future called PayPal and will fund a billion dollar company called Facebook will say, "Colleges are like the subprime mortgage lenders where people are being conned into thinking that this credential is the one thing you need to do better in life. And they're actually not any better off having gone to college; they typically are worse off because they've amassed all this debt."

My younger self, hear me out. You must become a voracious student of practical business skills if you are going to become a success because things are changing at a rapid rate and that rate of change will only increase in the future. I know that it seems impossible now, but I need for you to hear this.

In the future, people are going to stop using the Yellow Pages! I know it doesn't seem possible, but you must believe me. I'm begging you! Soon, when our family members are calling "from long distance," it won't matter because all of us will have unlimited long distance built into our cell phone plans! This is going to happen! I know it is almost impossible

Richard yet again proves the practical
value of his history degree.

to believe, but soon people are going to actually have cellular phones that aren't the size of a brick. My friend, nearly all of us will have more computing power in our phones than you have in that Micron computer you just purchased for $6,000. Clayvis, soon the World Wide Web will become known as the Internet and people will be able to log onto the Internet without hearing that insane nails-scratching-against-a-chalkboard screeching sound coming from their dial-up modem. I don't know if you can handle this next piece of information, but here it goes. In the future, people will even be able to log onto the Internet wirelessly from their cellular phones. I hope you're still conscious and reading after that one.

Listen man, you must learn how to build websites and optimize them so that other people can find your business when they are searching for the products and services they need. In the future, this skill alone will help your companies earn millions of additional dollars of gross revenue as you repeatedly beat your competition in the industries of cosmetic surgery, haircuts, fitness, spine surgery, dentistry, family medicine, public relations, speaking, online education, gourmet dessert and countless other industries. Clay, you must stop spending time memorizing facts about the Byzantine Empire and the nuances of Egyptian culture and you must begin scheduling 30 minutes per day to learn practical business skills. I know I told you this before, but it's worth repeating again:

- 88% of wealthy people read 30 minutes or more each day for education or career reasons vs. 2% of poor people.

- 86% of wealthy people believe in lifelong educational self-improvement vs. 5% of poor people.

(Stats taken from DaveRamsey.com based on research findings reported on Tom Corley's RichHabitsInstitute.com.)

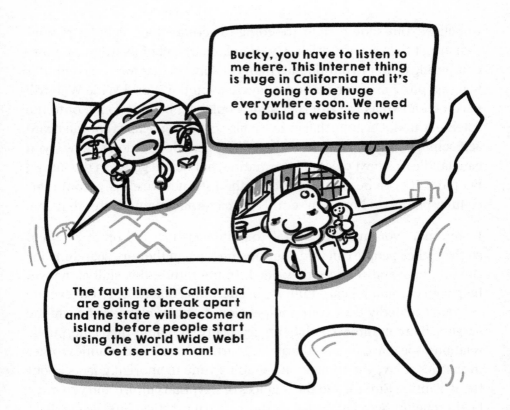

I'm going to ask you a few questions just to demonstrate how little you know about the practical things that actually matter, things that have the potential to make you more money, and how much you know about things that do not matter at all. Please answer the following questions:

- What is a permalink?
- What is the name of the two most famous members of the Wu-Tang Clan?
- How do you write a press release?
- Describe what photosynthesis is all about.
- How do you create a business pro-forma?
- What is the name of Q-Tip's #1 rap single and Top 40 hit?
- What is a Pitch Deck and how should you deliver one to venture capitalists?

- What was the batting average of the San Francisco Giants first baseman, Will Clark, during the 1989 season?
- What is your T-shirt / mobile entertainment company's profit per customer?

Clay, you have to wake up! In the future, just as it is now, most people don't block out the time to develop the jobs skills and mindsets necessary to find or create the jobs they want, so most people just settle for jobs they dislike.

- In 2014, Tami Luhby will write an article for CNNMoney.com called, "The American Dream Is Out of Reach." Research for that article will show that 59% of Americans in 2014 believe that the American Dream is not attainable.
- Research conducted by Gallup around that same time will show that only 13% of employees are mentally engaged at work. Once you have better Internet speed in the future, you can check out those statistics at http://www.gallup.com/poll/165269/worldwide-employees-engaged-work.aspx.

Success Is Guaranteed to Those Who Diligently Acquire Practical Skills

Why am I telling you all this? I'm telling you this because I know that YOUR SUCCESS IS GUARANTEED when you commit to learning and implementing practical and proven business success strategies. I also know that your failure is nearly guaranteed if you don't. The choice is yours, my friend.

You must stop wasting your time learning about things that do not matter to your future. You must spend more time learning about sales, marketing via the Internet, accounting, public speaking, motivation, overcoming adversity, how to raise capital, customer service, leadership and management. My friend, in the future you will build a website called www.Thrive15.com where thousands upon thousands of people from all around the world will be able to access all of this practical business education. But for now, you need to start reading and applying the concepts found with the books I've listed below. To make your life easier, I've put a note next to each book title and author to give you an idea why the book matters. Clay, every day that you choose not to live by the proven principles and success strategies found within these books, you will be forced to pay a "dumb tax" for your ignorance. I've said it before and I'll say it again: The choice is yours.

Richard doesn't find his new job very fulfilling.

"People who are unable to motivate themselves must be content with mediocrity, no matter how impressive their other talents." - Andrew Carnegie (A man who was obsessed with self-improvement and who became the second wealthiest man in the world after dropping out of school at age 14 to help his family make ends meet)

"People who are unable to motivate themselves must be content with mediocrity, no matter how impressive their other talents."

~ Andrew Carnegie ~
(A man who was obsessed with self-improvement and who became the second wealthiest man in the world after dropping out of school at age 14 to help his family make ends meet)

Think and Grow Rich by Napoleon Hill

This book has been read and endorsed by over half of the millionaires that you will meet before your 35th birthday. This was the book that inspired W. Clement Stone to found Combined Insurance, Oral Roberts to found Oral Roberts University, and countless millionaires to take their vision for their life to the next level. This book is the result of the most exhaustive research ever conducted into the success principles and mindsets of the world's most successful people.

How to Win Friends and Influence People by Dale Carnegie

Dale Carnegie's writings, courses and training schools are legendary. In fact, one of the world's wealthiest men, Warren Buffet, once said, "I actually have the diploma (from Dale Carnegie's School) in the office. I don't have my diploma from college, I don't have my diploma from graduate school there, but I have my Dale Carnegie diploma there because it changed my life."

Soft Selling in a Hard World by Jerry Vass

The best-practice sales strategies and systems found within this book will take your career to the next level. The secrets found within this book helped Maurice Kanbar (the man who founded Skyy Vodka) successfully market his real estate, helped a bakery triple their sales in 16 months, helped your photography company become the largest in your city, helped the men's grooming lounge business you are a partner in become sustainably profitable, and much more. Clay, THIS BOOK WILL CHANGE YOUR LIFE! No matter how good your current ideas are, if you do not learn how to influence other people to convince them that your idea is truly worth buying or investing in, you will never get where you want to go.

In the future, your online school called Thrive15.com will give people like you instant access to this type of powerful training without having to read all these books. However, until the year 2015 arrives when Thrive15.com launches, you are going to have to read like your quality of life depends on it - because it does.

I know what you are thinking, because I am you. I know the thought of reading all those books to mine for the nuggets of knowledge found within them sounds daunting. But until your video-based business school becomes a reality, just shut your mouth and read the books. My friend, if you promise to read those books immediately, I'll let you in on a little secret. In the future, you will partner with NBA Hall of Famer, David Robinson.

*You and David Robinson officially announcing to America that Thrive15. com has launched.

Yes, I'm talking about the future Hall of Fame basketball player David Robinson who will average 17.8 points per game during the 1999-2000 season! I told you, I'm from the future. I know this stuff. Look, you have to believe me! At the risk of destroying the universe by revealing information about the future, I'm going to give you a quick betting tip. David Robinson will win two NBA Championships - one in 1999 and one in 2003.

Currently in your world, there is no company in the marketplace employing an entire research, editing, production and graphic design team for the sole purpose of finding the world's proven success strategies so they can break them down into bite-sized, actionable 15-minute video-based training that humans actually enjoy watching because they are so engaging. But there needs to be one, and you are going to help build it. So kick the spirit of jackassery to the curb and start reading.

You must not let formal education get in the way of your practical learning. On June 12, 2005, Steve Jobs, the founder of Apple, will say, "The minute I dropped out of (college) I could stop taking the required classes that didn't interest me and begin dropping in on the ones that looked interesting."

Clayvis, you must start reading the following books as soon as they become available for purchase.

- Rich Dad Poor Dad by Robert Kiyosaki
- The E-Myth Revisited by Michael Gerber
- 21 Irrefutable Laws of Leadership by John C. Maxwell

- Guerilla Marketing by Jay Conrad Levinson
- Guerilla PR 2.0 by Michael Levine
- Scale by Jeff Hoffman and David Finkel
- Time Management Magic by Lee Cockerell
- The Service Profit Chain by James L. Heskett, W. Earl Sasser, Jr., and Leonard A. Schlesinger
- The Value Profit Chain by James L. Heskett, W. Earl Sasser, Jr., and Leonard A. Schlesinger
- Winning by Jack Welch
- As I See It by J. Paul Getty
- Born Standing Up by Steve Martin
- Built to Last by Jason Collins
- Good to Great by Jason Collins
- Crush It by Gary Vanyerchuk
- Do You by Russell Simmons
- Life and Def by Russell Simmons
- Eight Habits of the Heart – by Clifton Taulbert
- From Lucky to Smart – by Chester Cadieux

- In the Words of Great Business Leaders by Julie M. Fenster
- Made in America by Sam Walton
- More Than a Hobby by David Green with David Merrill
- Nuts! Southwest Airlines' Crazy Recipe For Business & Personal Success by Kevin Freiberg and Jackie Freiberg
- One Minute Manager by Kenneth H. Blanchard and Spencer Johnson
- Pour Your Heart Into It: How Starbucks Built a Company One Cup at a Time by Howard Schultz with Dori Jones Yan
- Purple Cow by Seth Godin
- Raving Fans by Kenneth Blanchard and Spencer Johnson
- Straight from the Gut by Jack Welch
- The $100,000 Club: How to Make a Six-Figure Income by D.A. Benton
- The Cashflow Quadrant by Robert Kiyosaki
- The Creature from Jekyll Island: A Second Look at the Federal Reserve by G. Edward Griffin
- The Gospel of Wealth by Andrew Carnegie
- The Education of an Accidental CEO by David Novak with John Boswell
- The Four-Hour Work Week by Timothy Ferris
- The Laws of Success In Sixteen Lessons by Napoleon Hill
- The Maui Millionaires by David Finkel and Diane Kennedy
- The Millionaire Next Door by Thomas J. Stanley, Ph.D and William D. Dank, Ph.D
- The Most Successful Small Business in the World by Michael Gerber
- The New Conceptual Selling by Stephen E. Herman
- The Ultimate Sales Machine by Chet Holmes
- Traction by Gabriel Weinberg
- Get Rich Click by Marc Ostrofsky
- The New Imperialists by Mark Leibovich
- The Slight Edge – Secret to a Successful Life by Jeff Olsen

- The Snowball: Warren Buffett and the Business of Life by Alice Schroeder
- The Art of the Deal by Donald Trump
- Radical Marketing by Sam Hill and Glen Rifkin
- Speak to Win: How to Present with Power in Any Situation by Brian Tracy
- Stand and Deliver – How to Become a Masterful Communicator and Public Speaker by Dale Carnegie
- Titan by Ron Chernov
- Who Owns the Ice House by Clifton Taulbert and Gary Schoeniger
- Your Best Life Now by Joel Osteen
- Pitching Hacks by Venture Hacks
- Pitch Anything by Oren Klaff

Tip from the future:

Clay, in the future a wealthy mentor will tell you, "Rich people have big libraries and poor people have big TVs."

Bernie invests in the biggest TV he can find.

CHOOSE A PATH

Clay,

I'm sorry about the tornado-like adversity that's been beating you up lately. I know it seems as though life may have dumped too much on you recently. Losing your best friend in a car accident, getting kicked out of college, getting married and attempting to start a business all within a span of 18 months would overwhelm anybody. But I want to encourage you by reminding you that you do have the ability to choose which path you are going to take with your life.

My younger self, you must listen to me: Remain diligent. Oprah Winfrey, the great producer, talk show host, entrepreneur, actor and media mogul who lifted herself out of poverty and the feelings of doubt and depression that swelled up within her after being abused, was correct when she said, "I believe luck is preparation meeting opportunity. If you hadn't been prepared when the opportunity came along, you wouldn't have been 'lucky.'"

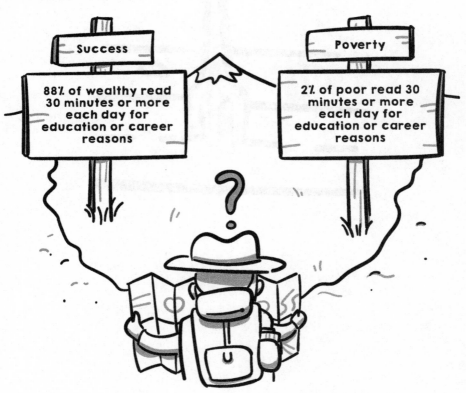

I am going to give you a drink from the fire hose of knowledge real quick to hopefully save you a few years of pain.

Rule #1 – To achieve success, you must determine your definite chief aim.

"Singleness of purpose is essential for success, no matter what may be one's idea of the definition of success."

~ Napoleon Hill (Author of Think and Grow Rich, the best selling self-help book of all time) ~

Rule #2 – To get paid, you must find a problem that the world has and solve it.

"Entrepreneurship and business success is achieved simply by finding a problem that the world has and is willing to pay to solve and then charging people for the solution."

~ Clay Clark (Former U.S. Small Business Administration Entrepreneur of the Year, America's self-proclaimed most humble man, and your older wiser self) ~

YOUR BUSINESS EXISTS TO SOLVE PROBLEMS
FOR YOU AND YOUR CUSTOMERS.
- CLAY CLARK
FOUNDER OF THRIVE15

Rule #3 – To get ahead and stand out in the game of life, you must do more than is expected.

"You can start right where you stand and apply the habit of going the extra mile by rendering more service and better service than you are now being paid for."

~ Napoleon Hill (The self-help author whose work made such a big impact on your life that you ultimately name your son Aubrey Napoleon-Hill after him) ~

"The average person puts only 25% of his energy and ability into his work. The world takes off its hat to those who put in more than 50% of their capacity, and stands on its head for those few and far between souls who devote 100%."

~ Andrew Carnegie (A man who dropped out of school at the age of 13 to begin working to help his immigrant family make ends meet) ~

Rule #4 – Be intentional about who you spend time with because the friendships you nurture will determine your connections, your sense of normal and your spending habits.

"Your network is your net worth."

~ Porter Gale (Bestselling author of the future and former Vice President of Marketing for Virgin America) ~

"41% said they landed a job through networking."

~ Susan Adams (Author of a Forbes article from the future titled, "Networking Is Still the Best Way To Find a Job" (June 7, 2011).) ~

"One of the challenges in networking is everybody thinks it's making cold calls to strangers. Actually, it's the people who already have strong trust relationships with you, who know you're dedicated, smart, a team player, who can help you."

~ Reid Hoffman (Part of founder team that will launch the billion dollar companies PayPal and LinkedIn) ~

Rule #5 – Don't be an idiot. Schedule time to learn or you'll end up being one of the 70% of Americans who hate their jobs.

"70% of Americans are negative about their jobs, Gallup study shows."

~ Beth Stebner, "Workplace Morale Heads Down," New York Daily News, June 24, 2013 ~

I'm not sure if I've shared these two stats with you two or eight times at this point, but I think you should see them again.

- "88% of wealthy people read 30 minutes or more each day for education or career reasons vs. 2% of poor."
- "86% of wealthy people believe in lifelong educational self-improvement vs. 5% of poor." – Stats taken from DaveRamsey.com based on research findings reported on Tom Corley's RichHabitsInstitute.com

Now, in fairness to you, I realize that this information may seem over-simplified, but work with me here. Steve Jobs once said, "Simplicity is the ultimate sophistication" and the legendary playwright William Shakespeare said, "Brevity is the soul of wit." I know your professors have spent the last two years saying, "Go ahead and write a 30-page paper in MLA format about this and then write a 60-page paper in MLA format on that," but you have to start asking yourself whom you should be listening to. Should you be listening to lifetime academics who have never left the campus to test their economic theories in the real world, who have told you that you if you will just earn your bachelor of science in this and your masters degree in that you will become successful? Or should you be listening to billionaire entrepreneurs like Peter Thiel and Steve Jobs?

Clay, you need to choose the path of success or you are going to choose the path of perpetual frustration by default. Benjamin Franklin said, "Some people die at 25 and aren't buried until 75." Don't die before you live, Clay. Choose to pursue your dreams and remember the Five Rules of Success I've included in this letter.

"Some people die at 25 and aren't buried until 75."
- Benjamin Franklin (U.S. Founding Father)

Sincerely, the You of the Future,

Clay Clark

P.S. Research shows that over 70% of people hate their jobs, very few people have anything saved for retirement and 59% of people don't believe that the American Dream is possible for them. Most people are wrong. The American Dream is entirely possible for anybody who is willing to put in the diligent and focused effort needed. My friend, it's a harsh truth, but most people are stuck where they are because they refuse to make the time to learn the practical skills they need and they are afraid to step out of their comfort zone to meet the people they need to know. This is jackassery, pure and simple, and you must begin to break free of this great cosmic habit force. Misery loves company so most people will tell you that you are crazy when you start embracing a world-view that is nearly opposite of the one they have. Don't waste your time arguing with jackasses; just move on. They'll end up working for you someday.

Jackassery ALERT: I could care less.

Most people say this all day without thinking. I used to use this phrase
frequently myself. The correct phrase is actually "I couldn't care less."
It is meant to express how little you truly care about something – you
care so little already, it is nearly impossible for you to care less. When
you say "I could care less," you are saying that you are not apathetic
about the topic at hand. You actually do care, but if pressed to do so,
you could care less.

"GREAT SPIRITS HAVE ALWAYS ENCOUNTERED
VIOLENT OPPOSITION FROM MEDIOCRE MINDS."
– ALBERT EINSTEIN
DEVELOPER OF THE GENERAL THEORY OF RELATIVITY

"I'm like a tree; I feed the branches of the people."

~ *Kanye West (A rapper and producer who consistently and unapologetically compares himself to Jesus)* ~

HUNT ELEPHANTS. DON'T CHASE RABBITS

Clay,

My man, I'm excited for you! You and Vanessa now have your first child and your jackassery appears to be in full remission. Although your entertainment business is really beginning to boom, I am here to warn you of problems that are coming soon.

Your mentors have told you that you'll have to completely change your thought diet if you don't want the forces of jackassery to start controlling you again. I know the thought of abandoning your roots to leave behind your life of jackassery seems overwhelming, but trust me, it's worth the change. Whenever you feel the urge to put your head into an audio toilet and pump it full of negative, hateful music, I encourage you to put your literal head into an actual public parks restroom toilet instead. I know that will feel gross and you might get several diseases, but at least you won't be damaging your mind. Remember, nothing is as powerful as a changed mind.

I'm spilling the beans early. Clay, you are eventually going to have five kids before your wife demands that you have a vasectomy. The vasectomy procedure is going to go badly and you are going to have a lingering injury. It's going to get bad. CLAY! It's going to get REAL BAD! I sincerely hope this freaks you out, as I enjoy messing with my former self (even though I know that means I'm actually messing with myself).

In the next few months, your thought diet is going to drift and you will begin to revert to the dark side. This episode of jackassery has the potential to really beat you up unless you take the advice of the billionaire entrepreneur T. Boone Pickens: "When you are hunting elephants, don't get distracted chasing rabbits."

What is T. Boone talking about? He's referring to this natural desire that we all have to begin chasing rabbits when the elephant we've been hunting is finally right in front of us. Now before you or a bunch of PETA members begin writing me letters, let me be clear that in the future, you don't become some safari-adventure big game hunter. Stay focused man. The "elephant" and "rabbits" refer to ambitions, not actual animals. Let me explain.

"When you are hunting elephants, don't get distracted chasing rabbits." - T. Boone Pickens (Self-made billionaire entrepreneur)

For some reason, humans tend to become somewhat fascinated by anything new. Throughout the next eight years of your life, you are going to see at least a dozen men you know leave their wives and children behind for "new" girlfriends and that initial excitement they feel when they are first being pursued by someone ten years younger than them. You are going to see countless business owners you know leave their profitable business models behind in search of some half-baked ambiguous business opportunity that promises to make them millions overnight. My friend, you yourself are going to be approached by someone with a net worth that looks great on paper. He is going to tell you what you want to hear and tell it to you in the way you want to hear it.

If this con artist were to approach you now, you would turn him down in a second. However, in a short period of time, you will have nearly stopped practicing the success habits that got you here. All the warning signs are going to be there, but you will fail to see them. At first you are going to be hesitant and skeptical of this person but over time, the lure of getting rich quick will wear you and Vanessa down and you will once again allow jackassery to rule you. Because the levels of jackassery in your

"The secret of success is constancy to purpose."
- Benjamin Franklin versus "Start-it-forget-it-and-move-on-Marvin"

blood will be so high at this time, things will get pretty bad and you will make a lot of poor decisions. This letter to you is my last-ditch effort to get you to change your course. I am hoping that you will be receptive to what I'm saying. After all, it's just weird to argue with yourself. Clay, you must be aware of these get-rich-quick scams. Please listen as I describe some of the worst types of get-rich-quick scams, some of which you will be exposed to in the coming months.

Rabbit / Scam #1 – If it seems too good to be true, it usually is.

Charles Ponzi (who was also known as Charles P. Bianchi, Charles Ponei, Carl, or simply 'The Ponz') told his investors that they would earn a 50% return on their investment dollars within a very short window of time. He was able to actually pay out huge returns to his initial investors because he was paying his past clients with the investment dollars of his new clients. He would then use the testimonials of his early investors as evidence of his success as a solid money manager. But when people started to sense that Ponzi's promises were maybe a little too impressive and they began to investigate his plan, things got bad quickly. Ponzi didn't have the funds to pay out when his investors called for their money. His scheme was exposed and he went to jail. Clay, way out in the future in 2008, Bernie "King of Jackassery" Madoff will be busted for operating his own Ponzi scheme, which will swindle his clients out of nearly $65 billion. There are plenty of other examples of this type of scheme, but what you need to remember is, if something seems too good to be true, it usually is. There is no substitute for time and effort.

Rabbit / Scam #2 – Beware of the SECRET Investment that Nobody Else Knows About.

Proverbs 13:11, from the New International Version of that highly offensive and controversial book known around the world as the Bible, says, "Dishonest money dwindles away, but whoever gathers money little by little makes it grow."

Over the years, you are going to personally witness countless close friends and family members who get caught up in a type of get-rich-quick investment scam that doesn't make sense. The con men ("snake oil salesmen") will look great at first and will always drive a nice car, have a nice family and all the right answers to your friends' questions. When people visit the homes of these con men, they will find Bible verses framed on the walls, fresh-baked cookies in the oven and potpourri in the bathrooms. The con men and their families will seem like great quality people. These men will be able to quickly convince your friends that their investment deal is related to a rare, short-term loophole recently discovered in "the system." This loophole is something that very few other people know about, which is why they will tell your friends that they need to invest the $20,000 now. These con men will encourage your friends to "keep the information to themselves" to "avoid the scrutiny from others who are too narrow-minded and just wouldn't understand." You will see your friends lose it all, as they decide to exchange long-term success for the promise of a short-term ludicrous return on investment. When you see these con men coming your way, run! Don't allow your inner jackassery, naiveté and lust to get rich quick talk you into spending even a moment with these people.

"Success is 10 percent inspiration and 90 percent perspiration."

~ Thomas Edison (The famous inventor who changed the world by inventing the first practical light bulb, recorded audio and recorded video) ~

Rabbit / Scam #3 – Beware Seminar Speakers and Sultans of Success

Over the next few years, you are going to be invited to speak at many seminars where you are going to meet some very rich people. The vast majority of the presenters you meet at these seminars will be honest, hardworking people who are sincerely motivated to help others. However, you are also going to run into some of the most manipulative and disgusting humans this planet has ever produced. These people are known as the "Get-Rich-Quick-Millionaire-Secret" people. Here are some tips in how to spot them:

Step 1 – They are going to try to convince you that you should come to their very cheap or free success seminar.

Step 2 – They are going to explain to you how you can get rich quick using their secret system, if you only have the faith to take action.

Step 3 – They are going to browbeat you with celebrity name-dropping or the promise of celebrity appearances. They want to adjust your emotional state, getting you and all prospective event attendees excited about the possibility of meeting some big-time celebrities and hearing them speak.

Step 4 – The seminar that they are going to present is going to be a marathon. They are going to try to isolate you from logical thinking for as long as possible so that you are mentally worn down when they finally do ask for massive sums of your hard earned money.

Step 5 – They are going to coach you through the process of raising your credit card limits. They tout this as "negotiation." You will be instructed on how to call your credit card company and what you must say in order to get your credit limit increased, which is then celebrated as a big win for you over the credit card companies that are "trying to take advantage of everyday consumers like you."

Step 6 – They are going to hard sell you a get-rich-quick course at the end of their presentation using a tsunami of fear-based and emotionally exhilarating hard close strategies, now that they know you have the appropriate credit limit to invest.

Step 7 – If you ever do make the mistake of actually paying to go to one of these courses in person, you will find that the slick speaker who originally convinced you to sign up for the course is not going to be there. You have been duped. The person teaching you was once taught by the guru himself, but you will soon discover that he has never made millions by applying the principles he was taught. No, the person teaching you is only making thousands now by scamming you.

Step 8 – Once they have convinced you to invest heavily in their programs and training courses, they will begin sharing their other "investment opportunities" with you. They will attempt to persuade you to trust them. Hopefully by that time, you will know enough to run away from their advice.

Step 9 – Their final step is to tell you that you have to apply for acceptance to their program because it is exclusive and not for everyone. This "give-and-take-away" move is incredible, because they are preying on your basic human need to want what you can't have. These people are soulless and slick. Watch out!

Rabbit / Scam #4 - Beware of Time Wasters Wearing Suits in Coffee Shops

As you begin to make more money, there will literally be hundreds of people salivating at a chance to screw you like a high-powered screw gun. These people are typically found wearing suits and hanging out in coffee shops. They are going to try to entice you with real estate deals "that no one else knows about," business ventures in Dubai, complicated currency swap plans and various ambiguous connections to fabulously wealthy Nigerian Bankers and other bogus sources of wealth.

The initial call you receive from them will sound something like, "Hey Clay, how are you doing? Man, I've been impressed following your success in the headlines. It's been fun to watch. Hey listen, we need to catch up. I specialize in working only with high net worth individuals like you and I would like to just sit down with you to see how I can help you achieve your goals. Let's grab some coffee and maybe I can learn a thing or two about you. How would tomorrow or Friday, around 10:00 AM or 11:00 AM either day, work for you? I'm excited to reconnect!" When that call comes, run! There is still time to escape.

Clay, I hope this message gets through your thick and beautiful skull and into your brain before the jackassery fills your mind with delusional optimism backed by half-baked facts delivered by a slick salesman.

Sincerely, Your future self,

Clay Clark

"I'M A GREAT BELIEVER IN LUCK, AND I FIND THE HARDER I WORK, THE MORE I HAVE OF IT."
- THOMAS JEFFERSON
3RD PRESIDENT OF THE USA

Nip it in the butt vs. Nip it in the bud.

A few years back, I remember laughing so hard, I literally choked on the water I was drinking when I heard an employee say, "This s%it stinks and I'm tired of dealing with him. We need to nip him in the butt, or I'm out of here!" I can only speculate that this employee was trying to communicate how frustrated he was that he was forced to continually deal with the same co-worker's problems. However, he was actually saying that something smelled terrible and so he felt compelled to bite a fellow co-worker in the gluteus.

CHAPTER 5

INVEST IN A MIRROR AND EVALUATE YOURSELF

"Face reality as it is, not as it was or as you wish it to be." - Jack Welch (Former CEO of GE)

Dear Clay,

Congratulations on all of the awards you've been winning and business success you've been experiencing. On a personal note, I know that you are concerned about the increased presence of hair found within your nasal cavity. You should be. In the future, this only gets worse. Pretty soon, you will have so much of this hair growing in your nose that you could harvest those nose hairs and weave them into a sweater each month if you wanted to. You are also going to reach a point where you will gain weight simply by smelling food. I know it's hard to believe, but it will happen. You will soon be spotted walking into restaurants plugging your nose and eating ice chips for lunch. It gets serious in your 30s man.

In the future, Anthony Tjan will be the CEO, managing partner and founder of the venture capital firm Cue Ball and the vice chairman of the advisory firm Parthenon. He will also co-author the New York Times bestseller Heart, Smarts, Guts, and Luck. In a Harvard Business Review article titled "How Leaders Become Self-Aware," he will say, "There is one quality that trumps all, evident in virtually every great entrepreneur, manager, and leader. That quality is self-awareness. The best thing leaders can (do) to improve their effectiveness is to become more aware of what motivates them and their decision-making" (July 19, 2012).

Daniel Goleman, psychologist and bestselling author of the New York Times bestselling book, Emotional Intelligence: Why It Can Matter More Than IQ, puts it another way, "If your emotional abilities aren't in hand, if you don't have self-awareness, if you are not able to manage your distressing emotions, if you can't have empathy and have effective relationships, then no matter how smart you are, you are not going to get very far" (New York: Bantam Books, 2005).

Clay, don't get me wrong here. Through pig-head discipline and determination, you have built a formidable event entertainment company that is regionally dominant, yet I know that your lack of self-awareness will serve as your Achilles heel if you don't address it soon.

With that in mind, I need for you to take five minutes and evaluate yourself on the following areas of business mastery. A rating of 10 means that you are a complete Jedi Master in an area. A rating of 1 means that you clearly have no competency and are figuratively standing naked in front of business associates every day in that area.

1. Your ability to manage your time and the increased responsibilities that come with being a leader.
   1 2 3 4 5 6 7 8 9 10

2. Your ability to raise seed, growth and venture capital.
   1 2 3 4 5 6 7 8 9 10

3. Your ability to create the standard "Pitch Deck" that most venture capitalists prefer.
   1 2 3 4 5 6 7 8 9 10

4. Your ability to create a detailed pro-forma so that you always know your break-even point, your hard costs, your variable costs, your cost of goods sold, your profitability per customer and the overall specific number of transactions you need to do in order to achieve your dreams.
   1 2 3 4 5 6 7 8 9 10

5. Your ability to optimize your website so that your company will appear at or near the top of Google searches.
   1 2 3 4 5 6 7 8 9 10

6. Your ability to design and launch effective landing web pages to improve your ratio of website visits to conversions.
   1 2 3 4 5 6 7 8 9 10

7. Your ability to market effectively using social media.
   1 2 3 4 5 6 7 8 9 10

8. Your ability to build a duplicable and scalable sales process.
   1 2 3 4 5 6 7 8 9 10

9. Your ability to train inexperienced sales people to become effective sales machines.
   1 2 3 4 5 6 7 8 9 10

10. Your ability to write effective sales scripts.

    1   2   3   4   5   6   7   8   9   10

11. Your ability to create an effective sales conversion pipeline.

    1   2   3   4   5   6   7   8   9   10

12. Your ability to teach your sales people how to overcome objections in a systematic and scalable way.

    1   2   3   4   5   6   7   8   9   10

13. Your ability to manage your sales people effectively.

    1   2   3   4   5   6   7   8   9   10

14. Your ability to create sales collateral and materials including effective business cards, brochures, print pieces, advertisements, etc.

    1   2   3   4   5   6   7   8   9   10

15. Your ability to launch an effective mailer / print piece campaign.

    1   2   3   4   5   6   7   8   9   10

16. Your ability to execute a successful tradeshow appearance.

    1   2   3   4   5   6   7   8   9   10

17. Your ability to lead a group of ten or more team members / employees.

    1   2   3   4   5   6   7   8   9   10

18. Your ability to think like an entrepreneur allowing you to spot the business opportunities that are all around you.

    1   2   3   4   5   6   7   8   9   10

19. Your ability to create and map out your customer service program in a scalable and duplicable way.

    1   2   3   4   5   6   7   8   9   10

20. Your ability to increase the overall level of quality of the products and services your company provides.

    1   2   3   4   5   6   7   8   9   10

21. Your ability to implement a mystery shopper program.

    1   2   3   4   5   6   7   8   9   10

22. Your ability to implement a merit-based program.

    1   2   3   4   5   6   7   8   9   10

23. Your ability to implement a profit-share program.

    1   2   3   4   5   6   7   8   9   10

24. Your ability to motivate yourself and stay motivated through times of great adversity.

    1   2   3   4   5   6   7   8   9   10

25. Your ability to create consistent media attention for your business.

    1   2   3   4   5   6   7   8   9   10

26. Your ability to lead what Gino Wickman calls a "Level 10 Meeting."

    1   2   3   4   5   6   7   8   9   10

27. Your ability to find, recruit, hire, inspire and retain top quality people.

    1   2   3   4   5   6   7   8   9   10

28. Your ability to know when to fire an employee.

    1   2   3   4   5   6   7   8   9   10

29. Your ability to design an appropriate compensation plan.

    1   2   3   4   5   6   7   8   9   10

30. Your ability to execute complex projects and tasks.

    1   2   3   4   5   6   7   8   9   10

31. Your ability to create, design and improve workflows.

    1   2   3   4   5   6   7   8   9   10

32. Your ability to say no to distractions in a tactful and consistent way so that you can stay focused on achieving your purpose.

    1   2   3   4   5   6   7   8   9   10

33. Your ability to turn your current business systems and processes into a duplicable and scalable turn-key business model.

    1   2   3   4   5   6   7   8   9   10

34. Your ability to make smart real estate decisions about buying, selling or leasing office space.

    1   2   3   4   5   6   7   8   9   10

35. Your ability to network effectively and turn interactions into active clients and friends.

    1   2   3   4   5   6   7   8   9   10

36. Your ability to manage the legal aspects of your business.

    1   2   3   4   5   6   7   8   9   10

37. Your ability to financially and emotionally navigate a lawsuit.

    1   2   3   4   5   6   7   8   9   10

38. Your ability to deliver public speeches.

    1   2   3   4   5   6   7   8   9   10

39. Your ability to lead effective workshops.

    1   2   3   4   5   6   7   8   9   10

40. Your ability to inspire people.

    1   2   3   4   5   6   7   8   9   10

41. Your ability to achieve a healthy and sustainable life balance.

    1   2   3   4   5   6   7   8   9   10

Congratulations, you have just completed an in-depth analysis of your business skills for the first time. As a congratulatory prize, I am attaching a real gift certificate to the men's grooming lounge you own in the future. Just rip out this gift certificate and feel free to use it during your first visit.

For first-time visitors only.

*Look dude, because I am you, I know you are thinking of mass-duplicating this gift certificate so that you can receive a lifetime of free haircuts at the Elephant in the Room (www.EITRLounge.com), just like you did during the great Dairy Queen Free Dilly Bar Counterfeit Coupon Scandal of 1998. Did you think that I (actually, we) would have forgotten about that by now? Well my friend, the truth is that your "move" was textbook jackassery / tomfoolery. I don't know what's more amazing, the fact that you literally made over 1,000 copies of those counterfeit Dairy Queen Dilly Bar coupons or that you redeemed them all, never got caught and didn't weigh 500 pounds from eating all that chocolate and ice cream.

I know that you are thinking to yourself, "Now that I've filled out this fabulous survey, what I am supposed to do with this information?" Well my friend, you must immediately begin to buy into the concept that what you don't know can and will hurt you in business and in life. You can't keep skinny-dipping in the shark-infested waters of business while wrapped in bacon without eventually losing a limb.

I know at this point in your life you have just started listening to internationally renowned business speaker and bestselling author Brian Tracy while driving to and from work, so you now know how valuable each and every word he says about business success truly is. Clayvis, let me give you a taste of some training you will soon hear that will blow your mind: "No one lives long enough to learn everything they need to learn starting from scratch. To be successful, we absolutely, positively have to find people who have already paid the price to learn the things that we need to learn to achieve our goals."

My younger self, listen, you beautiful man! Brian is saying that it is far easier and much less painful to learn from mentors than from mistakes. However, I know you and I know the way that your brain works. Getting through to you is about as easy as using an auger to drill down through 100 feet of dense rock. But I also know that once you finally shove a nugget of knowledge inside your gourd, it stays there forever. So let me hit you with yet another notable quotable on which you can marinate. This quote is from one your new favorite authors, John Maxwell. John says, "Growth demands a temporary surrender of security. It may mean giving up familiar but limiting patterns, safe but unrewarding work, values no longer believed in, and relationships that have lost their meaning."

Clay, I can sense it, you are experiencing an epiphany! You are starting to get it! You are starting to see that you are going to need to learn from mentors and not mistakes if you want to grow your business and your life exponentially. Sir Isaac Newton, the man we have to thank for the creation of calculus and much of the foundation for classical mechanics, once said, "If I have seen further, it is by standing on the shoulders of giants."

Clay, at the risk of ruining the entire space-time continuum and unraveling the very threads that bind our universe together, I'm going to give you a glimpse of the future. Until the year 2015, you must block off 30 minutes per day to read the books on the reading list I gave you earlier in my letters. However, in the year 2015 and beyond, you can log on to Thrive15.com to grab this information. As the rate of change in the world increases, the company you helped start will keep pace, pumping out more and more practical training at an even faster rate. Thrive15.com distills the books and knowledge you need to know into powerful and actionable training that will absolutely change your life once you begin to implement the principles, strategies and systems being taught. However, until Thrive15.com is a reality, you must learn from real mentors so that you reduce the number of mistakes you make.

I know connecting with a valuable mentor can feel like chasing down a unicorn at times, but it is possible. Here is the good news and the bad news. The good news is that after 60 days of continually calling, emailing, faxing, sending snail mail and Linkedin, Facebook, and text messages, you can usually reach 1 out of every 100 mentors that you target to meet. The bad news is that it will take you 60 days of continually calling, emailing, faxing, sending snail mail and Linkedin, Facebook, and text messages to reach 1 mentor out of every 100 mentors that you target to meet.

Clay, you are so close to escaping the death grip of jackassery. Now that you have the facts, you have to act.

"Most entrepreneurs are merely technicians with an entrepreneurial seizure. Most entrepreneurs fail because they are working in their business rather than on their business."

~ Michael Gerber ~

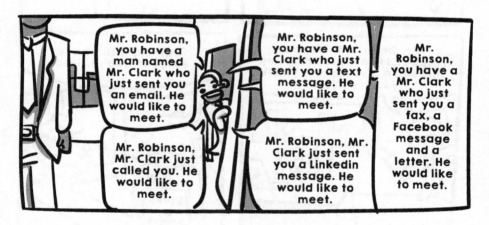

I say this with all due respect (once you say "with all due respect," you can say whatever you want – it's a universal law)...YOU MUST STOP BEING A JACKASS. You are enjoying some success, but you are capped and there's not a snowball's chance in hell that you will break out and achieve the higher levels of success you desire unless you choose to make a 180-degree life change right now.

I'm calling you out. When are you going to schedule time to learn the practical business skills and strategies you need to know? What are you going to start saying "no" to, in order to make time to learn? I dare you to take your life seriously enough to schedule 15 to 30 minutes per day to learn how to thrive in the world of business and in life. When is your

Darren experiments around the office with the phrase, "with all due respect."

"thrive time" going to be? Don't give me that crap about how you will have to get back with me after you pray about it. You and I know that you just say that when you don't want to make a decision, because once you say that you are going to "pray about it," most respectful people will never bring up the subject again. Keep in mind – I am not one of those respectful people.

ACTION IS THE REAL MEASURE OF INTELLIGENCE

Clay, if you don't schedule time to learn and begin to take your skill development seriously, it is going to cost you and your family millions of dollars in missed earnings. Your inability to optimize a website is one example of how much being ignorant is costing you. You must read, Get Rich Click by Ostrofsky as soon as it comes out. Beginning in 2015, log onto Thrive15.com to watch every video available dealing with search engine optimization. You must be intentional about learning these skills if you're ever going to get the job done.

Greg's roommates attempt to finally get their genius friend to work on time.

This is your year to thrive, my friend. You can do it, but you have to start blocking out time to learn more if you want to earn more.

Sincerely, You of the Future,

Boom!

Clay Clark

P.S. When your ex-girlfriend from high school reaches out to you randomly, do not introduce her to Vanessa (your wife). Introducing her to your wife is a bad idea inspired by Satan himself, the dark lord of jackassery.

Hey Clay, let me introduce myself, my name is Say-Tan.
You know your name sounds a lot like Satan...and your tail is red. Are you the Prince of Darkness?
No, my name is actually Luke E. Ifer, but my friends just call me Say-Tan. It's a nickname I've had since I got expelled from heaven....COUGH!!! I mean, since I moved here with my brother Kevin.
Great. Now that we've cleared that up, new friend, what advice do you have for me?
You need to introduce your ex-long term girlfriend from high school to your wife. I think they would become good friends.
Sounds great. I'll do that. Thanks Luke!

CHAPTER 6

HINT:
LOVE YOUR WIFE
THE WAY CHRIST
LOVED THE
CHURCH, NOT THE
WAY BERNIE LOVES
THE BOWLING ALLEY

Clay,

I want to make sure you know that no one is more dedicated to you and the idea of you getting it right now and in the future than me (which is actually you – try to resolve that one in your mind). So when I unleash the candor cannon on you below, I need you to read my words with a growth mindset, accepting criticism and not just seeking praise. I need you to start viewing your marriage as a sport and each day of marriage as a game that you must win.

WAKE UP CALL

You are currently treating your wife poorly. I realize that in the name of "providing for your family," you believe that working non-stop from 4 AM to 7 PM is a good thing. Clay, don't get me wrong here. Your diligence is a great thing; it is actually a superpower. However, you need to understand that all the work you're doing to earn a bunch of money

"In order to excel, you must be completely dedicated to your chosen sport. You must also be prepared to work hard and be willing to accept constructive criticism. Without one-hundred percent dedication, you won't be able to do this."
- Willie Mays (Twenty-four-time All-Star, Two-time National League MVP and Hall of Fame baseball player for the San Francisco Giants and the New York Mets)

does you no good if you're cutting your net worth in half every ten years by getting a divorce.

The incredible actor and comedian Robin Williams, whose personal struggles were well known, once said, "Ah, yes, divorce...from the Latin word meaning to rip out a man's genitals through his wallet."

YOU USED TO BE A ROMEO

Clay, before you married Vanessa, you used to chase her around everywhere. You would try to pick her up after her cheerleading practice at Oral Roberts University. You would call her dorm room and have one of those pointless "Hey baby, what are you wearing" calls. That call would usually last six hours and at no point did it have a point.

You would make out with her for two hours in a row until your bodies physically began to break down. You sent her flowers. You wrote her love notes. You kept getting busted checking her out whenever she walked by. You were like a hormonally imbalanced, though polite, dog in heat. You wanted her and you wanted her to know that you wanted her. She wanted to be wanted and she still wants to be wanted.

While you were dating, she knew that she was wanted because you wouldn't stop calling her, leaving her flowers, opening doors for her, taking her to the movies, going on walks with her, telling her how much you love her, agreeing to go shopping with her, recording songs for her and showering her with both material gifts and the ultimate gift of time (all the while fantasizing about actually showering with her). My friend, before you got married, you would have done just about anything to get her to say, "I do" so that you could do what you wanted to do for an hour or two. Don't act like you weren't thinking that. I'm you and I know that's what we were thinking.

YOU'VE MORPHED INTO A MAN-BEAR-PIG

However, after you said, "I do," you changed. You became a man-bear-pig, just as 90% of men do within two months of their wedding. Scientifically speaking, the transition from man to man-bear-pig is radical. To become a man-bear-pig, one must make a 180-degree change in values and pledge complete allegiance to the jackassery lifestyle. However, the actual metamorphosis takes place over a period of time so that most men do not even realize they are changing until it's too late. We usually don't notice that we have become man-bear-pigs until the wonderful woman we love points it out to us.

Where did that nose hair come from?

Age has not treated Clay Clark / Man-Bear-Pig nicely

Clay, you need to wake up. The drift-inducing habit force known as jackassery is eroding the strength of your marriage more and more with each passing day. I know you are rationalizing the decline in the quality of your marriage by comparing yourself to all the other couples around you, applying the ridiculously low expectations our cynical culture has for the institution of marriage. Consider this notable quotable from recording star Usher. When asked by Oprah why his marriage to Tameka Foster fell apart, he said, "I was faithful at heart, but not faithful all the way." He may be off when it comes to his understanding of what makes a healthy relationship, but then again, so is most of our culture. The dark force of jackassery is strong enough to rip nearly any marriage apart.

In the future there will be a song written and recorded by Andre 3000 of OutKast called "Hey Ya!", which will eventually become the most requested song at weddings. I have sent you the lyrics from the future so that you can see an example of the songs of a culture that endorses jackassery. Let's dive deep into the meaning of a portion of this song.

Andre Lauren Benjamin is better known by his stage name André 3000. He is a rapper, singer-songwriter, record producer and actor

You think you've got
Oh, you think you've got it,
But got it just don't get it, 'til there's nothing at all.

Translation: He is telling his girlfriend that although she thinks she is in control, ultimately she won't really understand what she has in him until their relationship ends.

We get together, oh we get together
But separate's always better when there's feelings involved.

Translation: He's saying that although they've known each other for a long time, it is better to separate when conflict and tension begin to arise in relationships.

If what they say is, "Nothing is forever"
Then what makes, then what makes, then what makes
Then what makes, what makes, what makes love the exception?

Translation: He is using the popular cultural mantra "nothing is forever" to justify his belief that committed relationships cannot possibly last. Rather than simply state his worldview, he asks you, the listener, a question. He inquires, if nothing lasts forever, then why would love be any exception to that rule? By employing the Socratic method here, he is hoping to stimulate critical thinking and illuminate your mind.

So why oh why,
Are we so in denial
When we know we're not happy here?...

Translation: He is now asking his girlfriend, "Why are we in denial of the reality that we are no longer happy?"

Translation Rebuttal: Commitment is at the very foundation of anything. If the CEO or founder of a company is not committed to lead his company through good times and bad times, the company is destined to fail. If the Founding Fathers had not been willing to die for their beliefs to guarantee all Americans the right to pursue happiness, then America would not exist. This whole concept of "do what feels good until it doesn't feel good anymore," also known as commitment-free living, is at the very core of the jackassery justification logic. This jackassery justification logic is used by people who seek to avoid experiencing the feelings of dissonance that naturally come when one takes actions that are not in line with one's stated worldview.

Y'all don't want to hear me,
You just want to dance

Translation: He is opining that you and all the people responsible for making this the MOST REQUESTED SONG TO BE PLAYED AT

WEDDINGS are not even aware of what the lyrics mean. Furthermore, you don't even care what they mean; you just want to dance.

The dark force of jackassery is so strong in our culture, that most people have never even seen a good marriage at work. Therefore, we compare our levels of jackassery with those of other men and marriages we see, rather than confronting the problem head on to eradicate this deadly condition.

To make sure you are tracking with me, I must give you a crude example to which I know you can relate. When you are working upstairs with your call center representatives, I know that you never notice when the room begins to smell horrific as a result of so many humans working so tightly packed together in a confined space (a "boiler room / call center"). However, every time you come back from your networking events, you always make a mental note about how terrible the room smells in comparison to the fresh air you have just been inhaling. This is how it is with your marriage. You don't realize how bad it has gotten because you're comparing your situation to all the other crappy situations around you.

Clay, trust me here. I have smelled the fresh air of the future. I have already gone to the deep, dark crevasse of crappy marriages and I have emerged from this hole, my friend! I have had to change nearly everything about my lifestyle to kill the man-bear-pig that I had become. If I could do it, you can do it, but it's going to take some honest self-evaluation and a commitment to change.

Remember when you first dated her...

She wanted to be wanted and she still wants to be wanted.

But now, you don't take her on dates, ever. Your entertainment company is growing virally and every event planner wants you to personally entertain for their event. Every Friday, Saturday, Sunday and holiday (except for Christmas) for the past seven years, you have DJ'ed a party for a paying client. You are going to have to learn to say "No," or you are going to kill your marriage.

She knew that she was wanted because you wouldn't stop calling her.

You never call her now because you are always working 14 hours per day.

You used to send her flowers.

Now, you only send her flowers when she is justifiably super mad about how much you've been neglecting her. Good job, jackass.

While you were chasing her around in the hopes of getting her naked (within the context of marriage), you constantly opened doors for her.

Now you say, "Hey, come on! Let's go! You need to hustle; we can't be late," because you are a man-bear-pig who has completely lost his sight due to jackassery-induced cataracts. Normal cataracts distort or cloud a person's vision, making light seem too glaring. Colors may not appear as bright as they once did. My friend, these jackassery-induced cataracts you have make you unable to see that you are being a complete jerk, even when presented with a high-definition, full-length video showcasing your man-bear-pig behavior and highlighting the overall impact that jackassery is having on your relationship with your wife.

You used to get dressed up and take her to the movies on a date night.

Now, you wear those "vintage" sweat pants the Oral Roberts University basketball team gave you 99% of the time while you sit at home. Instead of going out for date nights, you stay in whenever possible, because going out just requires you to eventually come back in anyway. Instead of going to the movie theatre, you now go online to see if you can find a movie that you two can watch at home. After looking for an online movie for about 34 seconds and not finding anything compelling to watch, you fall asleep on the couch by yourself, thus leaving your wife to conclude each night alone and frustrated over the fact that your once epic date nights have evolved to this. You are now a jackass inspired man-bear pig.

While you were salivating over her, you used to take her on walks.

Now, you work until 9 PM, come home and nose dive directly into bed.

While you were trying to get it on with her, you used to tell her how much you love her.

Now you say, "See you later, bye" and other surface level crap that typical acquaintances say. The heavy levels of jackassery in which you are now engaged seem to be affecting your hearing as well. You no longer hear yourself acting like a complete jerk.

While you were trying to convince her to say, "I do," you gladly agreed to go shopping with her.

Now you say, "Babe, just get whatever you want. I trust you. I'm going to crash and get a little sleep while you're at the store and we can hang out when you get back."

While trying to trick Vanessa into marrying you, you used to record songs for her and shower her with both material gifts and the ultimate gift of your time.

Now, you only do something special for her on cliché holidays like Valentine's Day and Christmas and you typically don't even do that until the very last minute.

You have to work so much because you are an ineffective delegator. And when you are finally forced to take something off of your plate, in perfect jackassery form, you just abdicate the responsibility, resulting in an epic disaster. Since I know you don't know, let me explain that "to abdicate" means you renounce or resign from your duties simply saying, "Screw it. I'm done messing with this. I don't care anymore! Now it's yours to handle, but I won't follow-up either. I simply just don't care about this at all anymore!"

Clay, you need to start delegating, which means to entrust a task or responsibility to another person. Then you must have the tenacity and the concern to follow-up to make sure that the task you assigned was completed properly and to the level of quality you expect.

Notable Quotable

"In God we trust; all others must bring data."

~ W. Edwards Deming (The electrical engineer, guest lecturer and management expert who is best known for the work he did with

the Japanese after World War II to help them become an industrial superpower. Many describe what he helped Japan do between 1950 and 1960 as a miracle. He literally helped Japanese manufacturers move out of the ashes of World War II to become the world's second largest economic superpower.) ~

The good news is that I'm sending these letters from the future, and I know that in the future, you eventually come around and become a decent husband. But I'm telling you that RIGHT NOW at this very moment, you are not helping yourself any. Just look at these statistics from Oprah's wingman, Dr. Phil.

According to Dr. Phil McGraw, Ph.D:

• 59 percent of marriages for women under the age of 18 end in divorce within 15 years. The divorce rate drops to 36 percent for those married

at age 20 or older. (Taken from "Cohabitation, Marriage, Divorce and Remarriage in the United States," written by M.D. Bramlett and W.D. Mosher. Published by the National Center for Health Statistics, Vital Health Stat 23(22). 2002.)

- 60 percent of marriages for couples between the ages of 20 and 25 end in divorce. (National Center for Health Statistics)
- 50 percent of all marriages in which the brides are 25 or older result in a failed marriage. (National Center for Health Statistics)

IT WILL TAKE AN ENCOUNTER WITH BLINDNESS TO HELP YOU SEE

Clay, why am I telling you all this? I'm telling you this because in the future, your son will be blind. I know this is hard for you to hear, but your son, Aubrey Napoleon-Hill Clark, will be born blind. Unfortunately, it will take his blindness for you to begin seeing what is truly important in life. You will experience a drastic shift in what you perceive as important. You will demonstrate your comprehension of this truth by honoring your wife and your family by scheduling time for them - just like you now do for the most important parts of your business.

In a controversial book called the Bible, which you personally do not currently read or believe, it says, "Husbands, love your wives, just as Christ loved the church and gave himself up for her" (Ephesians 5:25, New International Version). Notice, it does not say, "Love your wife the way Bernie loves the Bowling Alley."

Notable Quotable:

"Husbands, love your wives, just as Christ loved the church and gave himself up for her."

~ *Ephesians 5:25, New International Version* ~

You have some work to do in this area, my friend.

Your future self,

Clay Clark

ANYTHING THAT IS NOT SCHEDULED WILL NOT HAPPEN

"Time is the scarcest resource of the manager. If it is not managed, nothing else can be managed."

~ Peter Drucker ~
(Bestselling management expert and a man who has been called the founder of modern management)

Dear Clayvis,

I want to thank you on behalf of your wife and kids of the future for deciding to pull your head out of your gluteus maximus. I know that you are excited to see how much your life will improve now that you've decided to actually schedule time to take your wife on weekend dates, take your kids to the office when possible and schedule a weekly family time on Sundays for all of you to get together to grill and conversationally marinate. My friend, I can still sense the presence of a little jackassery buried deep inside your heart, mind and soul, but I know that you can kill it once and for all if you'll just focus on learning these last four lessons.

PROMOTION EQUALS MORE PROBLEMS
Success is beginning to happen for you. Your business ventures are all beginning to boom, but you cannot let this mean you revert to a life of jackassery by choosing to once again do everything yourself. In fact, you must do the opposite. You are going to be involved in a partnership with nine different companies even as you are the proud dad of five kids! You are about to experience massive growth in many areas of your life! Sorry to ruin the surprise, but your wife is going to have twins in the future. I know you thought that you were going to have another boy, but nope. You are going to have twin girls, Laya and Scarlett. Mentally marinate on that thought for a while. Five kids; four of them girls. Boom. In your face!

Because your life is going to get much more complicated, you must begin to simplify things and become an elite manager of time. Don't think you'll have to do this all on your own, though. In the future, you are actually going to partner with a legendary time management expert who is going to teach you what you need to know to become one of the elite time management experts on the planet. But why not take a sneak peak at some of these secrets a few years early?

I know this will blow your mind but Lee Cockerell, the former Executive Vice President of Operations for Walt Disney Resorts who once managed over 43,000 employees, is going to agree to become a mentor on Thrive15. com. Lee is actually going to teach the world via Thrive15.com, time management secrets that are simply not taught on the vast majority of high school and college campuses! Ken Blanchard, the legendary management expert and bestselling author of One Minute Manager and Legendary Service, has these good things to say about Lee's system: "The ideas in Time Management Magic (Lee's time management book of the future) aren't only for managers in the workplace, they're for everyone, every place! Here, Lee Cockerell shares his personal system that made possible his thriving executive career with entertainment and industry giants. Read this book to maximize your success in life!"

Younger Clay, I want you to read these points from the Five-Minute Time Management course that Lee Cockerell has put together. Read this twice. Then write out your answers to the questions that follow. Just because I know how you are, I'm going to suggest that you write each answer twice, just to drive the point home.

1. Schedule yourself to have planning time every day for 5 to 30 minutes.

   Questions:

   Are you scheduling 5 to 30 minutes per day for planning time? (This is a yes or no question, by the way.)

   When is your regularly scheduled planning time?

   Have you used this time for the past two weeks or more to plan your schedule?

2. Write down everything in your planner that you want to accomplish on a business, school or personal level.

   Questions:

   Do you have a central planner that you use to keep track of everything?

   Are you writing everything in your planner that you want to accomplish?

3. Ask yourself three questions every day: What did I not do well enough yesterday that I need to go back and work on today? What should I work on today, this week or this month that will not pay

off for 5, 10, 15, 20, 25 or 40 years? What personal responsibilities should I work on today (work, home, family, health, retirement, etc.)?

Questions:

Are you asking yourself these three questions every day?

When are you scheduling time to ask yourself these three questions every day?

4. The name of the game in managing your time and life is to THINK! Then get started.

   Questions:

   Did you schedule time to think today?

   When in your schedule do you intentionally set aside time to THINK?

5. Put a priority code next to each item in my planner. I use an " * " for items that are urgent, an "A" for items that are vital, a "B" for items that are simply important, and so on.

   Question:

   Are you putting a priority code next to each item in your planner?

6. When you get any free time, address the items marked " * " first until you finish the urgent tasks of the day. Then start the vital tasks that are coded "A." These vital things can be started today with something as simple as a phone call, but they may take six months to several years to complete. An example of a vital item might be to get into shape or get your MBA. Vital things may take a while to complete, but they have a big payoff (big bang for the buck theory). Next, you move to the items marked "B" – the important things, which are often routine but important nevertheless. These could be things like paying your tuition or doing the payroll. These tasks are important and need attention, but they are not urgent. Urgent tasks, to me, need to be addressed within a few hours.

Questions:

Are you really putting a priority code next to each item in your planner?

Do you have one centralized planner or are you attempting to implement the jackassery system of "planning" in which you write some to-do list items in your journal, some in your calendar at home, and some on your calendar at work?

7. Write down everything in your Day-Timer and carry it with you 24/7. When you make a commitment, write it down in the planner and then follow through.

Think before you add things to your planner. During your planning time, think about the different responsibilities in your life that you currently have or should have. For instance, I (Lee) think about my wife, my son and his wife, my three grandchildren, my job, my direct reports, my boss, my obligations to non-profit organizations I participate in within the community and church, financial planning for retirement, my health, my work partners, friends and parents. We all have responsibilities in our lives. Most people do not do a good job following through with them. If you make a list of your responsibilities and then think about them every day, you will be pleasantly surprised how much more you will get done in each area.

The list of responsibilities naturally grows as you get married or have kids or as you agree to take on additional responsibilities. This process of taking time to intentionally review your responsibilities is a great way to ensure that you have not forgotten anything to which you may have committed. If you will do this, you will find that you are more in control of your time and less stressed out. It does not matter how smart you are or what degree you have, if you cannot get things accomplished, success will elude you. Schedule your priorities right in your planner. Become the master of details and follow up. It is your reputation and YOU are responsible for protecting it.

Questions:

Are you writing everything down in your day-planner and using that planner 24/7?

Are you really writing EVERYTHING down in your day-planner?

8. If you want credibility as a leader, you must have a reputation for excellent follow-up, not only for urgent tasks, but also for those vital things in your life that make a big difference to you and others, and even in routine matters as well.

Questions:

On a scale of 1 to 10, with 10 being the highest rating, how would you rate your reputation for getting done what you say you are going to get done?

Justify your rating.

What action steps do you need to begin taking today to improve your time management skills, based on Lee's system?

Clay, don't over complicate this. Read Lee's rules again and begin implementing them right now. There is no other effective way to become a good manager of your time. Lee is one of the most organized, disciplined and results-oriented managers in the history of the planet. Take action today. The stress you feel right now will not decrease by itself.

"This is not about managing your time. It's about keeping your whole life under control. Plan the life you want or live the life you don't."

~ Lee Cockerell (Former Executive Vice President of Operations for Walt Disney World Resorts who once managed more people than you. So quit making excuses.) ~

If this is frustrating you, take it up with Lee in the future. I'm just here to share with you what he said. I know that truth hurts, but hopefully the pain of being an exhausted awful time manager will motivate you enough to actually take Lee's advice seriously. My friend, you must begin to adjust your schedule so that you can find time to grow your family, grow your business, sleep six to eight hours per night, and have intense level-10 sex every day.

Mystic Statistic

According to the research done by Tom Corley, bestselling author of Habits of the Rich, 44% of wealthy people wake up three hours before work starts vs. 3% of poor people.

Here's a Cliff's Notes version of Lee's tips:

1. You must have one day-timer and one to-do list for your one life.

2. You must assign the right priorities of urgent, vital or important to each item.

3. You must fight procrastination.

4. You must be mentally present at all times.

5. You must get started.

Here's a final prescription for you. In the future, Thrive15.com will give you access to one of the world's largest archives of notable quotables and words of wisdom from some of the world's biggest business successes. Take four of these Notable Quotables right now and see if the remaining symptoms of jackassery disappear by morning.

"Give me six hours to chop down a tree and I will spend the first four sharpening the axe."

~ Abraham Lincoln (A man who did not graduate from high school, whose life was filled with adversity as he lost eight elections, failed in business twice and lost three of his four sons before they became adults. When he became the 16th President of the United States, he worked tenaciously to end slavery and save the Union during the Civil War.) ~

Question: What axe (processes, policies and products or services) do you need to sharpen in your business so that it can become that much more effective?

"Lack of direction, not lack of time, is the problem. We all have twenty-four-hour days."

~ Zig Ziglar (Bestselling author of See You At the Top and a man who is revered as being one of the best motivational speakers of his time) ~

Question: Are you building enough planning time into your schedule to plan and prioritize your day or are you just reacting?

"There is nothing less productive than to make more efficient what should not be done at all."

~ Peter Drucker (Bestselling management expert, called the founder of modern management) ~

Question: What specific processes, policies and products or services do you need to eliminate altogether?

"The first rule of any technology used in a business is that automation applied to an efficient operation will magnify the efficiency. The second is that automation applied to an inefficient operation will magnify the inefficiency."

~ Bill Gates (A man who did not graduate from college, yet went on to co-found Microsoft and become one of the world's wealthiest people) ~

Questions: What specific processes, policies and products or services do you need to fix immediately so that you stop mass-duplicating failure? What specific processes, policies and products or services do you need to create to improve efficiency and overall productivity?

"People think focus means saying yes to the thing you've got to focus on. But that's not what it means at all. It means saying no to the hundred other good ideas that there are out there. You have to pick carefully. I'm actually as proud of the things we haven't done as the things I have done. Innovation is saying no to 1,000 things."

~ Steve Jobs (A man who did not graduate from college, yet went on to co-found America's most successful company, Apple. After being fired from the company he started, he bought PIXAR from George Lucas, the

man who created the Star Wars movies. With the release of Toy Story, PIXAR became the first commercially viable computer animation studio and movie house. After growing the valuation of PIXAR, Jobs took over Apple again and grew it into the world's most valuable company.) ~

Questions: What activities do you need to start saying no to right now?

Jackassery-In-Action Notable Quotable:

As the ultimate example of having enough courage to say something but not enough courage to act on one's convictions, Angus T. Jones of the hit show Two and a Half Men said, *"I'm on 'Two and a Half Men' and I don't want to be on it. If you watch 'Two and a Half Men,' please stop watching it and filling your head with filth. People say it's just entertainment. Do some research on the effects of television on your brain, and I promise you you'll have a decision to make when it comes to television, especially with what you watch."*

I made a complete 360-degree change in my life vs. I made a complete 180-degree change in my life

Oh, the bliss of being dumb! The splendor of being an oblivious mental midget cannot be accurately described with words, which is a good thing, since those afflicted by this terribly insidious disease called jackassery usually can't spell or speak well. I remember how simple things used to be before I became a student of life. I used to consistently run around saying, "I just hope that person A or person B will soon make a complete 360-degree change in their life." I meant to say that I wish the person in question would completely change in a positive and transformative way. However, I was literally encouraging them to spin in a complete circle before returning to their exact starting position, albeit with great enthusiasm.

CHAPTER 8

DEFINE.
ACT.
MEASURE.
REFINE.

Clay,

It appears that nearly all signs of jackassery are gone from your system. However, before we deep dive into this next principle, I want to call you on a recent act of jackassery, so dark that it is almost unspeakable. You boldly committed this dark act in the middle of the day at a local church, no less: You resorted to using a jackassery-inspired system to choose which judges to vote for in local elections. My friend, I know for a fact you went into the voting booth having no clue who each candidate was or what they stood for. You cast your vote based solely on whether the names sounded credible or not. Don't deny it! I was there. There you were saying to yourself, "Rodriguez...Rodriguez! He seems like a trustworthy guy. I'll vote for him. Now as for Thompson...I hate the name Thompson! I used to partner with a guy with the last name Thompson who really screwed me. So I am definitely going to cast my vote against Thompson. I hope Thompson loses."

To say that your system for choosing judges in local elections is dumb would be an epic understatement. It may, in fact, surpass Kanye West's idiocy when he said, "Sometimes people write novels and they just be so wordy and so self-absorbed. I am not a fan of books. I would never want a book's autograph." No. Kanye's statement still wins for being the premier example of idiocy in American history. But your system for picking judges is a close second.

Now that we've addressed your mindless voting process, let's move on. Here is the process to achieve entrepreneurial success in the business world:

Define. Act. Measure. Refine. What does that mean? Let me break it down for you like fractions.

DEFINE
When you are innovating, starting a business, or attempting to have success in the world of business, you must start with an educated guess - a hypothesis about the nature and source of the problem and your possible solution. Such a hypothesis must be based on observations of how your potential solution would appeal to likely buyers, be implemented

by your employees, and affect the problem both short and long term. When formulating your hypothesis, you must understand that it is not possible to experience success without first experiencing a few emotional and financial setbacks. Hypotheses are proven or disproven through time and application. I think Reid Hoffman, the founder of LinkedIn and one of the founding members of PayPal, explains entrepreneurship best when he says, "You jump off a cliff and you assemble an airplane on the way down."

ACT

Once you have formatted your hypothesis into an actionable plan, you must then take action in a methodical way. You can't study the issue so much that you are overwhelmed with options. This is commonly referred to as paralysis by analysis. The late, great success author Napoleon Hill said it best, "Action is the real measure of intelligence."

Clay attempts to get literal about testing Reid
Hoffman's theories on entrepreneurship.

MEASURE

When you take action as a businessperson, you need to measure the results. Was your hypothesis correct or not? Were you wrong? Don't get emotional, just measure the results and determine whether your assumptions and proposed solutions were correct or how you can improve next time. The inventor of the first fully functional light bulb, the inventor of recorded sound, the inventor of video, and the founder General Electric, Thomas Alva Edison once described his countless failed attempts to make a working light bulb saying, "I have not failed. I've just found 10,000 ways that won't work."

REFINE

If your assumptions were not correct, which is the case more often than not, then you need to learn from your mistakes, document your findings, pivot and take action on your newly refined potential solution. Bill Gates described this counterintuitive way of learning by saying, "Your most unhappy customers are your greatest sources of learning."

The true success process bears no resemblance to any of the following processes that you've attempted to use over the years:

Define. Define. Define. Define. – You can't just spend massive amounts of time speculating about what will work, my man. You need to invest the time needed to develop a detailed plan of what you think will work and then you have to take action quickly. After you have an educated guess in place, YOU MUST TAKE ACTION to get your business idea off the ground.

"Rarely do we find men who willingly engage in hard, solid thinking. There is an almost universal quest for easy answers and half-baked solutions. Nothing pains some people more than having to think."

~ Martin Luther King, Jr. ~

(Baptist minister, activist and leader of the African-American Civil Rights Movement)

"Action is the foundational key to all success."
- Pablo Picasso (Spanish painter, sculptor, printmaker, ceramicist, stage designer, poet and playwright whose great works of art are still talked about today)

Act. Act. Act. Act. – You can't just listen to Zig Ziglar and Tony Robbins motivational audio trainings all day while you're running around like a crazy man and hope success will find you. You first have to sit down and define the action items that will turn your big idea into reality, then get moving. To get you off the fence, I've given you three notable quotables to marinate on. If this doesn't get you moving, perhaps a weird encounter with a Taser or cattle prod are needed in your future.

"The path to success is to take massive determined actions."

~ *Tony Robbins (The most well known self-help speaker and author in the country)* ~

"You don't have to be great to start, but you do have to start to be great."

~ Zig Ziglar (Bestselling author and world renowned motivational and business speaker) ~

Measure. Measure. Measure. Measure. – You can't just run metrics and analytics reports all day and think the accumulation of knowledge will bring you success. All of your spreadsheets and data collection must be distilled into something that is actionable or it is just a huge waste of time. Stop collecting non-actionable data and stop listening to your teammates who love to fill the room with mindless statistics. Jack Welch, who was arguably one of the best CEOs of all time, talked about the importance of measuring what is going on within your business while still focusing on getting things done:

"One of my favorite perks was picking out an issue and doing what I called a 'deep dive.' It's spotting a challenge where you think you can make a difference...one that looks like it would be fun, and then throwing the weight of your position behind it. Some might justifiably call it 'meddling'...I followed up on all of them with a passion and a mania that often veered toward the lunatic fringe...To make the initiatives work, it took a passionate all-consuming commitment from the top. Beyond passion, there was a lot of rigor...Making initiatives successful is all about focus and passionate commitment. The drumbeat must be relentlessness. Every leadership action must demonstrate total commitment to the initiative...I was an outrageous champion of everything that we did, from our early need to face reality and change the culture to our major initiatives that reshaped the company. Whenever I had an idea or message that I wanted to drive into the organization, I could never say it enough. I repeated it over and over, at every meeting and review for years, until I could almost gag on the words."

Define. Act. Measure. Cry. Question the Meaning of Life. Cry. Refine. – Achieving success in the world of entrepreneurship and business requires you to have thick skin and an endless thirst for constructive, actionable criticism, not praise and false kindness. You must accept the fact that making mistakes is all part of the great game of entrepreneurship. Don't stop and question the meaning of life every time your business systems, processes or ideas fail to live up to your expectations. Just take the anger, frustration, disappointment and rejection you feel at that moment and plow them into that next level motivation you need to experience a big breakthrough right after your most recent breakdown.

"In times of great stress or adversity, it's always best to keep busy, to plow your anger and your energy into something positive."

~ Lee Iacocca (Former CEO of Chrysler, whom many credit with having saved the company from certain bankruptcy when he took over in 1979 making a salary of $1 per year) ~

"Temporary failures are a prerequisite to success."

~ Napoleon Hill (The bestselling self-help author of all-time) ~

Remember: Define. Act. Measure. Refine. You can do it. Don't let the dark cloud of jackassery insert doubt and fear into the equation.

Sincerely,

Your future self,

Clay Clark

P.S. Although you will never win a beauty pageant and you've never had an attractive man or woman compliment you for your rugged good looks, you and I secretly know that everyone wants your body.

Axe vs. Ask

One of the keys to jackassery is that you have to sound like a jackass in order to be perceived as a jackass. Otherwise, people will naturally assume that you are of average mental capacity. To ensure that you sound like a jackass, you must faithfully say the word "axe" every time you mean to reference the word "ask."

WITHOUT SALES, YOUR BUSINESS IDEAS WILL GO TO HELL

"Everything else becomes unnecessary in a business if nobody sells anything."

"I have always said that everyone is in sales. Maybe you don't hold the title of salesperson, but if the business you are in requires you to deal with people, you, my friend, are in sales."

~ Zig Ziglar ~
(Legendary self-help author, sales trainer and motivational speaker)

Clay,

I want you to learn this concept quickly, because it's a simple one: Without sales, your business ideas will go to hell. You see, Clay, unless you are from the federal government, you can't go around spending more money than you bring in, regardless of how good your idea is. I've heard that recently you ran for mayor and lost. If your political career ever turns around, you won't have to abide by the rules of balancing a budget, not operating at a loss, etc. But in the meantime, while your wife sits at home crying, having made the mistake of reading the incredibly insightful comments written about you by bold anonymous political enthusiasts, you must focus on sales.

*Living the American Dream...In 2007, I
ran for mayor of Tulsa and lost.*

"Sales? You mean I am actually going to stoop so low as to talk about sales when talking about business? What am I, dumb? Don't I know that nearly no business schools teach sales? Aren't I aware that most people would rather staple their inner thighs together than talk about sales?"

I hear you ranting, Historical Clay.

The beauty of these letters is that they are just between you and me (which is actually me and me). My friend, I know that very few people want to talk about sales, because it is more sexy to talk about corporate culture (not necessary without sales), vision (not necessary without sales), creating a transformative product (not possible without sales), or getting an MBA (not needed if you work for an organization where nothing is sold). They may not want to talk about it, but the reality is that "the sale" is oxygen to your business. Without sales, your business is dead on arrival.

Clay, you must go onto the Thrive15.com website as soon as internet speeds improve (trust me, this will happen – dial up is for suckers) and watch every video we have recorded on the topic of sales. You must learn the specific and technical skills required to sell and sell well. You must learn how to build rapport with your prospects. You must learn how to find the needs of your prospects. You must learn how to skillfully deliver information detailing how your company can uniquely solve the problems of your ideal and likely buyers. You must learn how to close deals. You must learn Jim Cathcart's incredible sales systems for upserving (a.k.a. upselling). You must learn how to isolate and overcome the objections of your potential buyers. You must learn how to make effective cold calls. You must learn how to set up a call center and you must learn how to build a scalable and duplicable sales system that even an idiot can implement.

Notable Quotable

"I try to buy stock in businesses that are so wonderful that an idiot can run them. Because sooner or later, one will."

~ Warren Buffet (Self-made billionaire known for being one of the world's most successful investors) ~

Clay of the past, until Thrive15.com becomes a reality for you, I need you to read the following books so that you can become a master of sales.

- Soft Selling in a Hard World by Jerry Vass
- The Ultimate Sales Machine by Chet Holmes
- Traction by Gabriel Weinberg
- Relationship Selling by Jim Cathcart

Don't let the small levels of jackassery still remaining in your system steer you away from certain success. Get those books. Read the books. Implement what you are learning as soon as possible.

"Procrastination is the bad habit of putting off until the day after tomorrow what should have been done the day before yesterday."

~ Napoleon Hill (The bestselling self-help author of all-time) ~

I know you can do it, my friend. You are making strides to completely free yourself from the poverty perpetuating pull of jackassery. Keep up the good work!

Sincerely,

Clay

Money is the root of all evil vs. The love of money is the root of all evil

Socialists and those suffering from involuntary vocalizations caused by jackassery often say, "Money is the root of all evil." However, the Bible (the book the culprit is attempting to reference) actually says in 1st Timothy, "For the love of money is the root of all evil" (1 Timothy 6:10, King James Version). The concept being expressed is that being in love with tangible currency in an Ebenezer Scrooge kind of way is not healthy.

CHAPTER 10

G.O.A.T.
+
B.O.O.M.
=
P.O.D

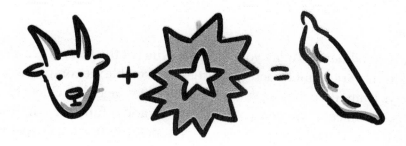

"Failure is a great teacher, and I think when you make mistakes and you recover from them and you treat them as valuable learning experiences, then you've got something to share."

~ Steve Harvey ~
(TV host, radio show personality and comedian)

Clay,

I have good news! Today you and your wife (of the future) are actually looking at various multi-acre properties to assemble the compound you've always wanted, including room for those silky cage-free chickens, fruit trees, an office, a kitchen your wife loves, and a fully-air-conditioned man room. The bad news, however, is it took you this long to get here.

My friend, if you will just invest the time to mentally marinate on this one simple concept I'm going to give you, you will avoid much pain while experiencing tremendous gain. Your friend and business partner David Robinson, who has over 30 years of experience in the NBA, puts the concept this way: "Mentorship is a pain-free way to learn."

I realize that in your younger years, you were extremely loyal to the jackassery practice of never asking for directions. I know that this refusal to ask for directions died hard when you got into that epic fight with your wife who correctly pointed out that because of your jackassery, it took your family over 16 hours to make the ten hour drive from Tulsa to Houston for Thanksgiving. I have noticed, however, that you are still not seeking

the advice of mentors as often as you should. For some reason, you are still committed to running blindly through the minefield of business rather than asking advice of the highly trained team that has already painstakingly combed the field for landmines. What is wrong with you man? Stop blowing yourself up all the time!

"Search for role models you can look up to and people who take an interest in your career. But here's an important warning: you don't have to have mentors who look like you. Had I been waiting for a black, female Soviet-specialist mentor, I would still be waiting. Most of my mentors have been old white men, because they were the ones who dominated my field."

~ Condoleeza Rice (Former Secretary of State during the President George W. Bush administration) ~

Here is the secret sauce:

G.O.A.T. + B.O.O.M. = P.O.D.

Greatest	**B**ig	
Of		**P**ossibilities
	Overwhelming	
All	+	**O**ptions =
	Optimistic	
Time		**D**reams
	Momentum	

Clay, any time you want to learn something in any area of your life, go out and find someone who already knows the answers to the questions you are asking (that's your Greatest of All Time / G.O.A.T.). Once they tell you how to solve the problem, you must go out and actually implement the prescribed action steps as quickly as possible with big overwhelming optimistic momentum (B.O.O.M.). If you do this, you'll create the possibilities, options and dreams (P.O.D.) you are looking for.

Do not overcomplicate this. Just do it. In the future, you achieve exponentially bigger success than you ever thought possible because of this principle. That's what Thrive15.com is all about. It's about giving everyone access to answers from the G.O.A.T.s of business so that Thrivers can achieve the P.O.D.s they are looking for. All Thrivers have to do is supply the B.O.O.M.! In the future, you will notice that every successful entrepreneur and business owner you interview for Thrive15.com is obsessed with this concept, although they may call it by different names. They are all obsessed with getting the answers they need from people who have already paid the price to learn what they need to know to get where they want to go faster.

Implement this system and I promise you will make more money faster than you ever have before. If you don't implement this system, I'm going to come back into the past and fight you.

Boom!

Clay of the Future

"No one lives long enough to learn everything they need to learn starting from scratch. To be successful, we absolutely, positively have to find people who have already paid the price to learn the things that we need to learn to achieve our goals." - Brian Tracy (World renowned speaker and bestselling author)

Conversating vs. Conversing

"Conversating" is not actually a word, but it was definitely a non-word that I used all the time in place of the correct word, "conversing." A hallmark of practicioners of jackassery is the authoritative and persistent use of non-words.

CHAPTER 11

ONLY STOP LEARNING WHEN YOU STOP BREATHING

Clay,

It's been a few months since your last flare up of serious jackassery, but I worry. At any moment you could relapse, so promise me you won't ever stop studying people who are more successful than you. I've only shared this stat with you 602 times throughout the course of these letters, but I worry that you might have forgotten it already so I'll repeat it again here. According to research conducted by bestselling author Tom Corley for his book, Rich Habits – Daily Success Habits of Wealthy Individuals, 88% of wealthy people read 30 minutes or more each day for education or career reasons vs. 2% of poor people.

Clay, there is a notable quotable I want to share with you from Carol Dweck, Ph.D, the bestselling author of Mindset: The New Psychology Of Success. She says:

"What on earth would make someone a non-learner? Everyone is born with an intense drive to learn. Infants stretch their skills daily. Not just ordinary skills, but the most difficult tasks of a lifetime, like learning to walk and talk. They never decide it's too hard or not worth the effort. Babies don't worry about making mistakes or humiliating themselves. They walk, they fall, they get up. They just barge forward. What could put an end to this exuberant learning? The fixed mindset. As soon as children become able to evaluate themselves, some of them become afraid of challenges. They become afraid of not being smart. I have studied thousands of people from preschoolers on, and it's breathtaking how many reject an opportunity to learn."

Clay, listen to me. Jackassery is buried somewhere deep inside all of us and we can only minimize its harmful effects on our lives if we have the courage to look deep within and identify our inner jackass.

Clay, don't make me come back in time to beat you savagely for being stupid, because I will figure out the technology if I have to. But if for some reason I can't figure out how to come back in time to fight myself, rest assured that life will kick the crap out of us now, which will cost us a fortune in the future. Being dumb is expensive, my friend.

Remember, it's up to you to apply and share this knowledge I've sent back through time through these magical letters. You must spread this message. If you know of someone who is struggling under the influence of the painful and wealth-repelling habit force known as jackassery, give them a copy of these writings before it's too late. My friend, we all know the world doesn't need another Clay Clark-style jackass.

Sincerely,

Your recovering jackass self of the future,

Clay Clark

CPSIA information can be obtained
at www.ICGtesting.com
Printed in the USA
LVOW03s1753010917
547220LV00001B/4/P

9 780998 443508